This Book Belongs To

_____

BLACK MOTHERS

SONGS OF PRAISE
AND CELEBRATION

KRISTIN CLARK TAYLOR

GRAMERCY BOOKS / New York

This 2006 edition is published by Gramercy Books, an imprint of Random House Value Publishing, by arrangement with Doubleday, both divisions of Random House, Inc., New York.

Gramercy Books is a registered trademark and the colophon is a trademark of Random House, Inc.

Random House
New York · Toronto · London · Sydney · Auckland
www.randomhouse.com

"Mother-Maps" by Laura Randolph Lancaster reprinted by permission of Johnson Publishing Company, Inc.

Book design by Jennifer Ann Daddio

Printed and bound in the United States of America.

A catalog record for this title is available from the Library of Congress.

ISBN: 978-0-517-22954-5

10 9 8 7 6 5 4 3 2 1

*This book is dedicated to my children, Lonnie Paul Taylor II and
Mary Elizabeth Taylor, for making me a part of the miracle
of motherhood, and to my husband, Lonnie, without whom
our little "miracles" would not have been possible.*

—KRISTIN CLARK TAYLOR

Acknowledgments

First and foremost, thanks be to God as I embarked on this wonderful journey of a book. His grace and goodness stirred my soul and my mind in miraculous ways. His protective embrace kept me buoyant throughout.

To my ever-supportive husband, Lonnie, you are my gift from God. Thank you for your sturdiness and strength, and to my children, Lonnie Paul and Mary Elizabeth, for their patience and for the quiet pride that I know they hold in their mother.

I thank everyone who sat down with me to talk about their mothers for this book: They are the embodiment of their *own* mothers, full of soul, compassion, and generous spirit. To my five sisters and one brother, thank you for making my child-hood so bright and rich with memories; memories that I hope shine through in this book.

I'm also grateful to Maja Keech, with the United States Library of Congress, for welcoming me with open arms into the Library's photographic collection and, in doing so, lending texture and visual weight to this project. To my photographer, Jason Miccolo Johnson, I will always admire not only your calm spirit and keen eye, but your magical ability to keep my two squirming, restless children still for so many hours as we shot the book cover.

And to the angels who walk among us, Sister Ann Forrest of Mount Carmel House in Washington, D.C., and Mike Young, program director for "For the Love of Children," thank you both for your heightened sense of selflessness and spirituality and for all that you do for African-American women everywhere who are struggling to get their lives back on track.

To my sister-friends who wrap me up in their love and make my heart shine. Thank you for your support and laughter: Karen Gaddis, Lola Keyes, Nancy Kleinman, and Novellia Pounds; gems, all of you.

This book could not have been written without the help and constant support of my agent, Madeleine Morel, and my editor Janet Hill, a strong, spiritual woman of words who is passionate about her craft and refreshingly modest (perhaps even unaware) of the rare wisdom she carries deep within her.

This book has been a spiritual journey. To those of you who traveled with me, I will always be grateful.

Kristin Clark Taylor

Contents

God cannot be everywhere,
so he created mothers.

—ANONYMOUS

INTRODUCTION

A black mother is a precious gem. She is as brilliant as a diamond; as deeply hued as bronze. Her legacy is as richly veined as the finest marble in the world. All that she has given to us, her children, is more precious than gold. This book celebrates and glorifies black mothers everywhere.

It lifts them up and casts them, luminously, into the rich limelight they deserve. Our mothers deserve to shine. The image of the black mother, her smile, the sparkle in her eye when she laughs, the feel of her cool, assuring hand on our feverish foreheads, should enlighten our lives and illuminate our memories as brightly as the North Star. This book thanks our mothers for their wisdom, their words, their undying strength, and for the memories they've created and preserved in each of us; memories that will live forever.

My own earliest memories of my mother have to do with her humming. When she hummed a song in our bright yellow kitchen on Woodland Street, it lit up my entire little world. The "mother sounds" she created swirled all around our kitchen and throughout our house, wrapping themselves around the banisters of our stairs and weaving themselves through the fabric of our family life. I savored the clean, rustling sound of her starched cotton dress, simply because I knew it meant she was turning from the stove to bend down and scoop me up into her arms. At an early age, I experienced the joy of motion as it had to do with Mother; the sheer rapture I felt when she'd pick me up, settle me onto her hip, redistribute the weight of her small body, and turn back to the stove all in one fluid motion—to finish up dinner.

Although I didn't realize it then, my mother was giving me all that I needed and all that I would ever need: Love. Nurturing. Attention. Warmth. That safe, soft place in the graceful curve of her neck that I could nuzzle while she hummed and cooked. The inescapable, everlasting richness of a mother's love. The *anticipation* of being scooped into her arms—knowing that any moment, any second, I'd be pulled up through the air toward this beautiful, bronze woman who was my *mother*—was as sweet as the scoop itself. It was not only love but the promise of *her* love that so brightly illuminated my little world.

And how I'd cling to her! Happily, hungrily, like a small, brown papoose. I was the youngest of her seven brown papooses; constantly, purposefully being nurtured in our comfortably chaotic household of nine people.

It is because of Mother that I write this book. The hip she placed me on. The songs she hummed to me. The tears she kissed from my cheeks when I was hurt or sad (*never* wiped; *always* kissed). I write this book to celebrate every African American mother who ever kissed a scraped knee, broke up a playground fight, spent part of the rent money on a pair of badly needed Buster Browns, preserved a memory, instilled in her young one an everlasting image of racial pride, or encouraged in her child imaginative, courageous thinking. I write this book in praise, celebration, and profound thanks to black mothers everywhere who guided our feet and showered us with the sweet, syrupy, unconditional love that has sustained our spirits, enriched our lives, opened our hearts, and kept us strong. To the heroic black mothers who have withstood pain and indignity, suffering and sacrifice—all for the good of their children—this book praises your existence and your memory.

A word on the book's format: *Songs* is a collective, shared celebration of the black mother, a love song that will be sung by many voices. I am indebted to all the people who sat down to remember their mothers with me, who shared their stories and opened their hearts. I am also grateful for being able to draw from other works, other voices, and other authors who are passionately eloquent on the subject of motherhood. This collaborative process enriched and enlarged the everlasting beauty of the women who brought us into this world. The collective memories and shared images in this book magnify the majesty of mother-hood and the ancient, inextricable bond that exists between the black matriarch and her child. This book encompasses not only my story but many stories. It is not a solo performance, but a joyful, harmonious *choir* of voices which will join in this ringing celebra-tion.

And finally, ultimately, praise be to God Almighty. He has blessed me richly and bountifully with a strong spirit, faithful friends, and close family. He has guided my hands as I've created this book. But, perhaps more than anything else, He has blessed me uniquely and magnificently by making me part of the miracle of motherhood. To have brought forth new life into the world, to have nurtured growing life inside my body, and to have acted as the vessel—the portal, if you will—through which my own children passed is a miracle of such magnitude that it takes my breath away. Being part of this miracle has taught me humility. It has taught me life lessons that I will never forget.

Lessons that have to do with humming and with hugging. Like my mother, I hum to my children all the time. Like my grandmother, I hold my children closely, in a warm, lingering embrace. And like all of our mothers, I try to instill in my children the pride of our racial heritage and the dignity of our cultural past.

This is too joyful a journey to take by myself. It requires collective celebration. So come with me. Sing praise. Uplift your voices. And as you open this book, open your hearts as well. Prepare to give thanks. Prepare to place our mothers—all of them—on bright, shining pedestals.

For that is exactly where they belong.

KTaylor

ONE

GIVER OF LIFE

And God blessed them, saying,

Be fruitful, and multiply.

—*Genesis 1:22*

At every child's birth, a mother is born.

As a mother, I have twice been "reborn." Each time, the process was nothing short of miraculous. My mother, Mary Elizabeth Clark, was still alive while I was pregnant with my firstborn son, Lonnie Paul. We'd sit in the late afternoon sun together, talking about the miracle of life and babies. She would tell me about her own experiences bringing seven children into the world; how I was colicky when I was born; how rubbing cod liver oil under my sister's chin when she was three days old helped cure her cold. Her stories, to me, were shining golden nuggets of wisdom, which I gobbled hungrily. I listened intently when she spoke; I wanted to absorb her every word. Ironically, as I was methodically preparing for the arrival of new life, I should have also been preparing for the suddenness of death: Mother died six months after Lonnie Paul was born.

Initially, I saw her death—particularly as it related to my infant son and my new role as mother—as a cruel, bitter twist of fate: God was trying to teach me that life and death are inextricably, intertwined. I began to realize that God was right; life and death *are* intertwined—and in that knowledge there was no longer pain, but beauty and comfort. With the birth of my son and the death of my mother— dramatic, life-changing events that occurred in such rapid sequence—I came to understand and appreciate that I had been made part of the cyclical, universal motion of motherhood. I had been made part of the miracle of life.

When my daughter, Mary Elizabeth, was born two years later,

Mother wasn't there with me, standing at the kitchen sink, showing me how to give her a bath. She wasn't there to whisper gentle words of guidance and comfort as I struggled with our newborn daughter. But God is good that way: He'd *already* allowed me to fully absorb the life lessons that Mother taught me before she left. And over time, He'd placed within me the everlasting knowledge that motherhood and the concept of mothering never really stops. It lasts forever, even if we do not.

Black mothers leave a legacy of strength and sustenance for their children. It is part of who we are, and who our foremothers were. If we listen very closely, we can still hear their words of wisdom, and in listening, comes learning. We can *learn* to be good mothers. We can learn to nurture our newborn or yet-unborn babies. And because we want to be as strong for our children as our mothers were for us, we can learn, over time, to sway gracefully with the universal motions of motherhood.

The rhythm within us is intrinsic.

—KCT

To my Precious Little One:

Never had I imagined that I'd question my judgment in my decision to venture into motherhood. I have long known that this was one of life's greatest joys that I wouldn't allow myself to miss. But because my impending role of *mother* has preceded my role as *wife*, I've been forced to ask myself, "Am I the proverbial unwed black mother?"

Never mind that I'm all grown up and have earned a respectable place in society, complete with a career, real estate and a loving man in my corner. Are others watching my growing belly and thinking "what else is new?"

I share this with you only because you, too, will have cause to question your judgment many times in your life. And sometimes it will be merely because of the color of your skin and all the perceptions that brings.

But even as I teach you to say "please" and "thank you" and all the other lessons of childhood, I'll teach you to have strength and conviction in all that you do; to know from within why you've chosen your path and to trust your motivations implicitly.

Then, when you're inevitably labeled by those who know no better, you will not love or believe in yourself any less!

With all my love and admiration,

Mommy

—CELESTE A. JAMES,
IN A LETTER WRITTEN
TO HER UNBORN CHILD

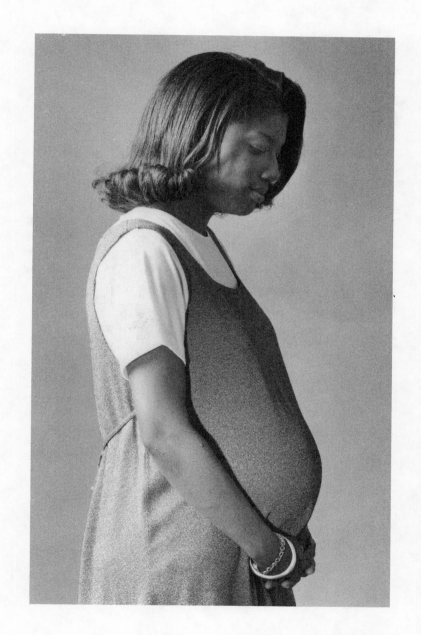

THE MOTHER'S BLESSING

Hope and joy, peace and blessing,
Met me in my first-born child.

—FRANCES WATKINS HARPER,
A FOUNDING MEMBER OF THE NAACP

A baby is someone just the size of a hug.

—ANONYMOUS

When I was most sorely oppressed I found solace in his smile. I loved to watch his infant slumbers; but . . . I could never forget that he was a slave. Sometimes I wished that he might die in infancy. God tried me. My darling became very ill. I had prayed for his death, but never so earnestly as now I prayed for his life; and my prayer was heard. Alas what a mockery it is for a slave mother to try to pray back her dying child to life! Death is better than slavery.

—HARRIET JACOBS, SLAVE

The woman about to become a mother, or with her newborn infant upon her bosom, should be the object of trembling care and sympathy wherever she bears her tender burden or stretches her aching limbs . . . God forbid that any member of the profession to which she trusts her life, doubly precious at that eventful period, should hazard it negligently, unadvisedly or selfishly.

—OLIVER WENDELL HOLMES

For thou hast possessed my reins: thou hast covered me in my mother's womb. I will praise thee; for I am fearfully and wonderfully made: marvelous are thy works; and that my soul knoweth right well.

—PSALMS 139:13-14

. . . Wife and child,
Those precious motives, those strong knots of love.

—WILLIAM SHAKESPEARE

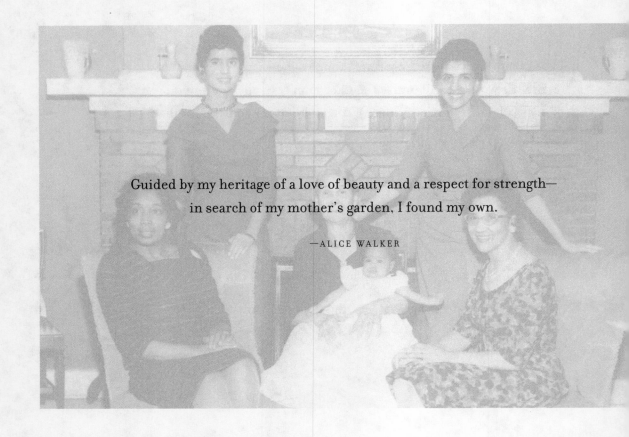

Guided by my heritage of a love of beauty and a respect for strength—
in search of my mother's garden, I found my own.

—ALICE WALKER

Blessed are you among women, and
blessed is the fruit of your womb.

—LUKE 1:42

This is the reason why mothers are more devoted to their children
than fathers: it is that they suffer more in giving birth and are more
certain that they are their own.

—ARISTOTLE

O God, guide my hands in the delivery of this child. Steady my nerves
and focus my mind, sharpen my instincts as I help bring this child
into the world. Ease the pain and fear of the mother and the anxiety
of the father with anticipation and joy in springing forth new life.

—MARIAN WRIGHT EDELMAN

I hope that people appreciate their mothers. And I also hope that a lot of the young, black girls who *become* mothers recognize the magnitude and importance of the job that they have. People need to realize—young women in particular—that parenting skills are developed over the course of a lifetime. And it takes at *least* that long to raise a child correctly.

—BENJAMIN CARSON, M.D.,
DIRECTOR OF PEDIATRIC NEUROSURGERY,
JOHNS HOPKINS HOSPITAL

I am an only child. One of the reasons my parents give me for that is that I was a painful birth. I weighed over ten pounds and was 22 inches long. My body grew so quickly that I had to wear leg braces when I was two . . . The doctors actually wanted to break both of my legs to straighten them out . . . My mom said, "You're not breaking my baby's legs." And that was that. Even doctors feared my mother.

—GRANT HILL

When a woman is in labor, she has pain, because her hour has come.
But when her child is born, she no longer remembers the anguish
because of the joy of having brought a human being into the world.

—JOHN 16:21

My mother sang with me in her stomach; I sang with Bobbi Kris in
my stomach. I believe the child starts to develop within, and whatever is put inside of you—whatever you read, whatever you think,
whatever you do—affects the child.

—WHITNEY HOUSTON

Some Jamaican women look to their dreams to tell them if they are pregnant: Dreams with lots of fish or ripe fruit in them are considered a positive sign of pregnancy. Our Egyptian sisters contend that dreams can also tell you if you're having a boy or a girl: Dream about a headkerchief and it's a girl; a handkerchief and it's a boy!

—DENNIS BROWN, M.D.,
AND PAMELA TOUSSAINT

When you were born, our lives lit up. You dusted away all our cobwebbed corners and breathed fresh air into our lives. I remember looking down at you and thinking, "Yes, yes. God is good."

—VELMA CHILDS,
ON THE BIRTH OF HER
DAUGHTER, CORRINA

Jesus love me! This I know, for the Bible tells me so;

Little ones to Him belong; they are weak, but He is strong.

Yes, Jesus loves me, yes, Jesus loves me

Yes, Jesus loves me, for the Bible tells me so.

—A HYMN THAT SHOULD BE SUNG (OR HUMMED)

BY EVERY BLACK MOTHER, TENDERLY,

TO HER INFANT

When I was pregnant for the first time, I developed this "quick list" of the ten most important things a black mother can do as she prepares to give birth to her child:

1. PRAY. Ask God to impart upon you the wisdom of our maternal forebears. Pray to the child inside you; for his development and maturation and for his soul to be at peace. Shower upon him the infinite power of God's love. Bring God close in around the two of you.

2. LISTEN. To yourself. To the inner movements of your body. To other black mothers, especially your own, who have words of wisdom to share. To your mate, who may need you during this time more than he's actually letting on.

3. MOVE. Exercise your body. Tone and strengthen your muscles. Physically prepare yourself for the dramatic transformation into motherhood. Keep your daily diet healthful and balanced.

4. LEARN. From elderly black women who have walked this road ahead of you. From books, articles, and resource guides that can offer expert advice on the childbirth experience. From other black mothers who did it right; and from those who did it wrong.

5. REJOICE. Spend time actively giving thanks for being made part of the miracle of motherhood. Let your baby know that his or her very *existence* brings you unspeakable joy.

6. NURTURE YOUR PROTECTIVE INSTINCT. All mothers protect their young. Begin figuring out, early on in your pregnancy, how to protect your child from the ravages of racial and cultural discrimination. Begin assessing ways to bring cultural and racial pride into the heart of your little one. Maintain, protect, and continue the legacy of racial dignity and cultural pride that your own mother worked so hard to keep alive for you. Let the fact that outside of your warm womb lies a cold and sometimes cruel world spur you into protective action.

7. BE POSITIVE. While you are pregnant, surround yourself with positive, life-affirming people. Create comfortable places where you and your family can exist peacefully, harmoniously. Lift yourself and hoist your spirit above the negative. Like a growing flower, always turn toward the sunlight. To naysayers and negativity, say, "Get back!"

8. GIVE. Of yourself, to those who are in need. Generosity nurtures a healthy spirit.

9. REMEMBER. Those mothers who came before you but are no longer alive. Draw strength from their memory, and let that strength flow freely toward your baby.

10. FEEL. Freely and without reserve, experience the love and tenderness you feel toward your baby. Even if your baby is still

growing within you, send strong feelings and thoughts conveying how much you cherish him. Skeptical that your unborn baby won't receive these messages of love? Not to worry. I promise you. He will.

—KCT

There are two ways to live your life.
One is as though nothing is a miracle.
The other is as though everything is a miracle.

—ALBERT EINSTEIN

Black mothers-to-be:
Choose to believe that the child growing inside
of you is nothing short of a miracle.

TWO

Spiritual Anchor

And the child grew and became

strong in spirit, filled with wisdom;

and the grace of God was upon him.

—Luke 2:40

As a child, Mother brought God straight into my home and into my heart.

Every morning before I left for school, she'd kneel down, place her cheek against my cheek, and say something comforting like, "If God is with you, who can be against you?" It was Mother who brought God in close around the two of us before I walked out that front door every morning. And I wore His love proudly, wrapped around my little shoulders like a protective cloak, all suited up in my coat of divine and impenetrable armor, ready to meet whatever the day had to bring.

When black mothers bring God into their children's lives, they are lovingly, purposefully, placing rich, velvet cloaks around their little shoulders. When we create and maintain a healthy spirituality in our children, we are letting them know that God loves them, and that God *is* love. There is no more powerful or lasting a lesson to teach our children—for in letting them know that they are the object and recipient of God's love, we teach them to love themselves and we gently nudge them toward the comforting realization that they will forever be protected by His watchful gaze.

I pray with my children every day—around the dinner table, before we leave the house, when trouble is near, and in the midst of happiness. In our home, God is our constant. My husband and I work diligently, quietly, to let our children know that He is with and among us always. He is accessible at all times. Black children need to know that. They need to be made actively aware of God's everlasting goodness and infinite mercy.

To black mothers who praise God with their children and their families, praise be unto *you*. To our mothers who cradled us in their loving arms and tenderly opened our hearts to God's goodness, we thank you. To the spiritual beacons who shined their lights into our lives and taught us that there *is* a place to turn when the going gets rough and He *is* our lifeline in turbulent, stormy seas, praise be unto you. To every mother who ever pulled a roll of Life Savers from her purse during church service and allowed us to pop one quietly into our mouths so that we would listen to Pastor preach the Word more carefully, we thank you.

Don't we owe our children that? Don't we owe them the comforting knowledge that, for the rest of their days, they'll never, ever have to walk this road alone?

—KCT

BLACK MOTHERS

As for me and my house, we will serve the Lord.

—JOSHUA 24:15

My mama's favorite scripture? From Matthew 10:29–31: "Not even a sparrow, worth only half a penny, can fall to the ground without your Father knowing it. And the very hairs on your head are all numbered. So don't be afraid; you are more valuable to Him than a whole flock of sparrows." And because my mama told me this, I knew that it was true. God's love for me is infinite.

—ANONYMOUS

Do I believe I'm blessed? Of course I do! In the first place, my mother told me so many, many times, and when she did, it was always quietly, confidently.

—DUKE ELLINGTON

He will turn the hearts of parents to their children.

—MALACHI 4:6

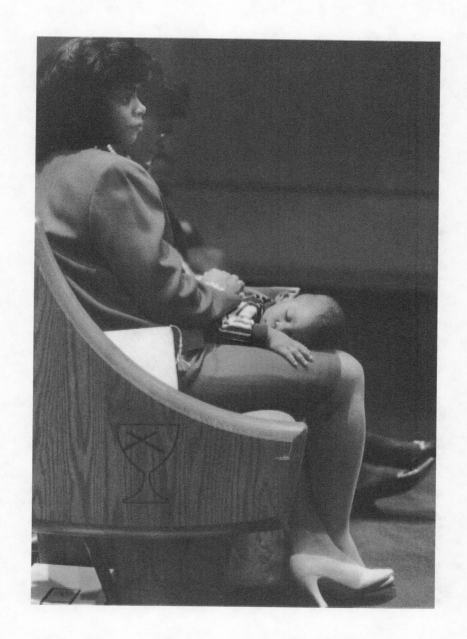

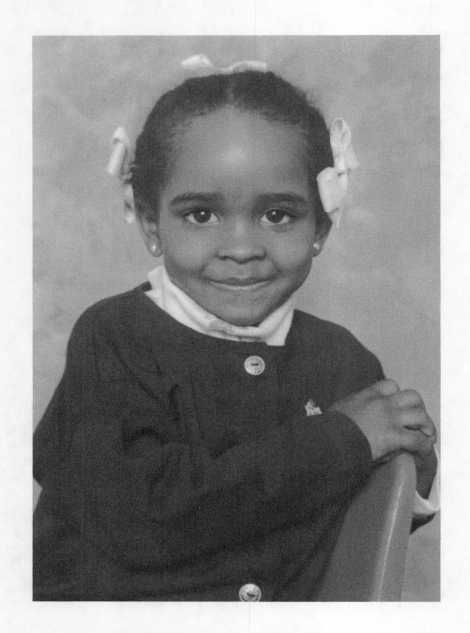

BLACK MOTHERS

Dear Mommy,

What does God look like? Is he black? Is he white? Long hair or short hair? Whatever he looks like, I know that he is always around us and guiding us in his shining path. I know that God is with us all the time, especially in church. Eating breakfast, he's there. In the car, he's there. At school, God is there, and while we are asleep, God is there. I know that God gives a lot of people strength, I just can't name them all. I bet you I will remember all the things about God and Jesus that you and Daddy tell me to remember.

One thing that I will never forget is once Daddy and Lonnie Paul were sleeping and you woke me up early in the morning while it was still dark out and asked me, "Do you want to go to church with me?" I said yes. So we got dressed up and went to church. At church the pastor says "God is good," then we say, "All the time!" My favorite part is when we switch parts and the pastor says "All the time," then we say, "God is good!"

God is *so* good.

And he is good all the time.

—MARY ELIZABETH TAYLOR,
IN A LETTER TO HER MOTHER,
KRISTIN CLARK TAYLOR

. . . the four of us kids sat on the second row right behind Dad, who was sitting on the front row with the deacons. Mom sat across the aisle in the third row. She told me she had no particular reason for sitting there other than the fact that she just liked that seat. But the location allowed her to keep her eyes on the back of our necks . . . The sermons touched my eight-year-old soul. The cadence, the rhythm, the flair was exhilarating. The minister would gradually build up to a high emotional pitch and then in a repetitive fashion give the congregation the message they had come for: "He's a Rock in the Weary Land!" "He's a Shelter in a Mighty Storm!"

—JAMES COMER, M.D.,

MAGGIE'S AMERICAN DREAM:

THE LIFE AND TIMES OF A BLACK FAMILY

We always arrived early for church, which began at 11 A.M. Between rising and then, there were eight baths to get and your Sunday-go-to-meeting clothes to don. No less important, there was one of my mother's unforgettable breakfasts to enjoy . . . When our pastor evoked the poetry of the Psalms, his melodic voice was sweet as honey . . . Heads nodded and paper fans stirred the heated air . . . Our mother, a small, demure woman whose outward sweetness belied her resolve, never shouted either, but tears would roll down her cheeks.

—JOHNNIE COCHRAN, JR.

"How can I see God?" I would ask Mother all the time. She would always tell me: "Look about you and you shall see Him playing with your children. And look into space; you shall see Him walking in the clouds, outstretching His arms in the lightning and descending in the rain. You shall see Him smiling in flowers, then rising and waving His hands in the trees." I loved hearing her say this because it was comforting and affirming for me to visualize God walking in clouds and playing with children (I always envisioned him playing with black children). Much later, I realized she was quoting from *The Prophet*, by Kahlil Gibran. But by then, Mother had died. Coming across those words again made my heart sing. It also made me cry.

—KCT

Ev'ry time I feel the Spirit movin' in my heart
I will pray
Upon de mountain my Lord spoke
Out of His mouth came fire and smoke
Ev'ry time I feel the Spirit movin' in my heart
I will pray.

—NEGRO SPIRITUAL

The prospect of being baptized scared me to no end. Because I was afraid of the water, I hadn't learned to swim. I wanted to be a Christian but I didn't want to drown doing it . . . I knew this baptizing was gonna kill me for sure . . . by the time the day and place of my baptism arrived, Reverend Bruce was ready and able to perform the duties of his cloth. Or, so he thought, until he encountered one terrified six-year-old Deloreese Early . . . The water in the baptismal pool came up to Reverend Bruce's waist. I was barely taller than his knee. I knew there was no way I wasn't going to drown.

When he finally carried me into the water, me kicking and screaming and splashing, he tried to reason with me. "I won't let you fall, just hold onto me!"

"I know you're gonna drown me!" I screamed and screamed.

"Don't you want to be a Christian and give your life to God?"

"Yes I do, but you might drop me and I will drown!" I kept screaming.

He prayed, he begged, he cajoled, he pleaded.

In the middle of a huge, long scream, I saw Mama come to the side of the baptismal pool and give me one of those looks I knew said: *"If you keep embarrassing me, if he doesn't drown you I will kill you personally myself!"*

And as she looked that look dead in my eye, she said to me in no uncertain terms, "Get baptized or get out of there!"

While I was looking at my mother, Reverend Bruce dunked me. I was wet, cold and shaking all over. But I was baptized.

—DELLA REESE

THANKS, MOTHER

I never could tell you Mother,
The words were never there,
To say how much I love you,
To thank you for your care,
To let you know my thoughts,
I tried a million times,
Words have not been written,
That let my feelings rhyme,
Your tender love has guided me,
Your wisdom makes me strong,
From encouragement I try again,
When everything goes wrong,
You see the words are written,
They are simple, but so true,
Thanks for letting *me* be *me*,
And *thanks* for being *you*.

—MRS. WILLA GASTON, NINETY-TWO,

WRITTEN IN REMEMBRANCE OF HER MOTHER

And the child grew and became strong in spirit, filled with
wisdom; and the grace of God was upon him.

—LUKE 2:40

My mother taught me that my talent for singing was as much God's work
as a beautiful sunset or a storm that left snow for children to play in.

—MICHAEL JACKSON

A Christian must keep the faith,
but not just to himself.

—MOTHER TO HER CHILD

Next to God, we are indebted to woman, first for life itself, and then,
for making it worth living.

—MARY MCLEOD BETHUNE

*The joy of celebrating God's goodness with our children
is boundless. It defies gravity in that it allows our children
to soar like eagles and stand with their feet planted
firmly on the ground; both at the same time.*

THREE

POWERFUL PROTECTOR

❧

She girds herself with strength,

and makes her arms strong.

—Proverbs 31:17

My mother was a petite, beautiful brown woman who glided gently into rooms and crossed her legs at the ankles "just so" when she was drinking afternoon tea. The sleeves of her dress always seemed to blow and sway softly around her; warm summer breezes, especially when we'd all sit on the front porch at night, made her look like a bronzed angel in the moonlight.

And although I was secretly enchanted with the way the wind would gently lift her skirt or blow her hair, and was mesmerized by the way the slanting rays of the late afternoon sun would make her forearms all golden and warm as she bent down to tie my Buster Browns, I knew instinctively that every ounce of her grace and softness could quickly transform itself into the darkest, rolling thunderstorm if circumstances dictated. I am certain that I knew my mother's softness. And I am equally certain that I knew her strength—particularly if she sensed that any of her seven children were in danger.

As a child, I knew beyond a doubt that Mother was my fiercest protector. If Mother was close by (and even if she wasn't close by), I felt utterly secure in the knowledge that no harm would come to me. This knowledge gave me strength, courage, and a spectacularly heightened sense of self-worth.

Isn't that the knowledge that all African American mothers need to infuse into our children? I believe it is. We need to instill in our children the indisputable knowledge that we—their mothers—are their constant protectors and renewable resource. How do we impart this knowledge? Not in large, splotchy chunks or dramatic displays of maternal bravado, but almost as though we were administering an IV to a young patient—in slow, steady drops so that it fills their system, their minds and their hearts, from head to toe.

My own children know that I would risk—even give—my life for them, in the same way I knew it of my mother. I don't shout it from the rafters of our home, but I do administer intravenous spiritual feedings to my children on a regular basis. I feed them slow, steady drips of my raw, maternal, fiercely protective instinct. And as long as they're receiving my maternal serum, it's not really that important to me that they realize they're being fed at all.

Black mothers are like that—as are *all* mothers: sweet as syrup one minute and, when necessary, sharp as a dagger the next. Our maternal thunderstorms rumble deep within all of us. And as vital as that dynamic is, so also is knowledge that our children realize, with clarity and conviction, that their mothers are there for them. No matter what.

—KCT

My mother . . . is soft-spoken and easy going . . . She taught me that I should feel a sense of "somebodiness" but that on the other hand I had to go out and face a system that stared me in the face every day saying you are "less than," you are "not equal to." She told me about slavery and how it ended with the Civil War . . . She made it clear that she opposed this system and that I must never allow it to make me feel inferior. Then she said the words that almost every Negro hears before he can yet understand the injustice that makes them necessary: "You are as good as anyone." At that time, Mother had no idea that the little boy in her arms would years later be involved in a struggle against the system she was speaking of.

—MARTIN LUTHER KING, JR.

Strength and honour are her clothing; and she
shall rejoice in time to come.

—PROVERBS 31:25

I've faced some challenges in my lifetime trying to provide for my children. I was on public assistance for a while. There were times when I just didn't have enough money. I had to make ends meet the best I could. The money that I did get was just enough to pay bills. You know how peer pressure is: The kids would come home talking about "this person has this" and "that person has that"—I had to deal with all of that. I remember when my son was small, Jordache jeans were the hottest thing out. He just *had* to have a pair of Jordache jeans. So you know what I did? I went out and bought him a pair of regular jeans and *told* him they were Jordache jeans. He'd come home and say, "Ma, the kids at school say these aren't Jordache jeans!" And I said, "Reggie, you know what? You can name your pants anything you want. They're your jeans and because of that, they're special!" Well, it worked. After that, I couldn't pull that boy out of those jeans.

—LINDA MYRICK

My mother had a very difficult life. As a child, she was bounced around from home to home and ended up living with different relatives. She was one of twenty-four siblings. She married at age thirteen, trying to escape her environment. She discovered her husband was a bigamist. She didn't have any education. She had no resources. But through all of that, she never felt sorry for herself. She never felt victimized. She always felt like there was something she could do to somehow gain control of her life. She believed that as soon as you started acting like a victim, then you became one. Never once did she feel sorry for herself. The unfortunate thing for my brother and me was that she never felt sorry for us, either! It really didn't matter what was going on: You were not going to get a sympathetic ear from her. She'd simply say, "Well, do you have a brain?" And of course my answer would be, "Yes, Mom." "Then you could have thought your way out of that," she'd answer. "You could have figured out a way to solve that problem!"

—BENJAMIN CARSON, M.D.

BLACK MOTHERS

I remember well how my mother often hid us all in the woods, to prevent master from selling us. When we wanted water, she sought for it in any hole or puddle . . . full of tadpoles and insects: she strained it, and [passed] it round to each of us in the hollow of her hand.

—MOSES GRANDY, A SLAVE WHO ESCAPED
TO ENGLAND AND DICTATED HIS
AUTOBIOGRAPHY THERE

My mother never gave up on me. I messed up in school so much they were sending me home, but my mother sent me right back.

—DENZEL WASHINGTON

My children and I faced very difficult times early in life. They sometimes had to skip school so that I could wait for the welfare check to come so I could run out and buy food. Or I'd sometimes have to send them to school late—after the check was cashed—so that they could eat first. They'd have to tell their teachers they were sick, because I really couldn't let the teachers know the real reason they were staying home. I refused to send my children to school hungry.

—PAULA WHARTON-LITT

It was my mother who was dragged from work and down to school whenever one of us was in trouble and was getting jammed by the principal . . . We could not have hired a better advocate for all the money in the world. She stood up to the principal like no other mother I knew, and ran interference for her children whenever she thought we weren't getting a fair shake.

—MONTEL WILLIAMS

My daughter Lola recently told me that she appreciates all of the things I do to protect her. She says that so many of the things that I do are "courageous." Because I didn't seem to have fear, she says *she* didn't have fear. What this means is that, as her mother, I have given her strength. I have given her courage. She now believes that she has the strength and the courage to succeed because her mother made her *not* afraid. I jump hurdles and confront obstacles for my children because my own mother gave me unquestioning, undying love. Growing up, I knew that my mother was my fierce protector, because there were just some underlying givens: her love for me, her belief in me, and in the absolute knowledge—in my mind and in my heart—that if I were in trouble, she would come for me. As a child I remember my mother saying to me, when I was facing danger or trouble, "Hang on, Snoopy. Just hang on." And I knew that I would be all right. The beauty of this whole "protective" process is that, in my family, it is multigenerational. My mother continues to lay herself down not only for me but for my children. In my family, there are multiple, living layers of maternal protective instincts. Black mothers have to give this to their children. Our children must know that, in time of trouble or strife, we will be there for them. My son, B.J., is the fire in my soul. I say to him all the time—before a game, for instance—that if anything goes wrong, I'll run out onto that field in a hot minute. I'll run for my children. Just like my mother ran for me.

—LOLA KEYES

I've come a long way. I have two children, three grandchildren. I'm a mother and a grandmother. I'm in recovery, and I've been clean for almost five years. Raising children during this time—especially when I had to be physically separated from them because of my circumstances—was so hard. I've been through the mill and through the ringer. In and out of transitional shelters and homes. We're struggling today, but we're making it, step by step. I'm doing the best I can with what I got. My children know I'll watch over them no matter where I am or what I'm doing. My daughter, she is my cub. And I am the lion, watching over her. She'll always be my cub. And I'll always be right beside her or somewhere close, protecting her. Just like a lion.

—VALINDA EPPS

This is my beloved, and this is my friend.

—SONG OF SOLOMON 5:16

Stand by your own children,
and suffer with them till death.

—HARRIET ANN JACOBS, SLAVE

You're worried about whether the teacher will yell at you for defending yourself? Why worry? I'd just go home and tell my mom and she'd take care of it real quick. My mom doesn't play *around*.

—TAYLOR'S SON, LONNIE PAUL,
TO A FRIEND, OVERHEARD
ON THE SOCCER FIELD

When the heat was off, I'd sleep in my coat. My momma was more inventive. She would heat up the iron, wrap it in a towel, and put it by our feet. If it was the water that was cut off, Bubba would go out to the backyard, find the main line and turn it back on. Then we would fill every bucket and tub we could find.

—GLADYS KNIGHT

As my mother had done for me, I told my son jokes and encouraged him to laugh at himself. The black child must learn early to allow laughter to fill his mouth or the million small cruelties he encounters will congeal and clog in his throat.

—MAYA ANGELOU

Mama's entrepreneurial spirit was never far beneath the surface. She always had a dime squirreled away for a crisis; ran her own dairy for a while, and was never without an idea about how to manage in a crunch . . . Like Mama, I have always wanted to earn my own dime.

—MARIAN WRIGHT EDELMAN

The doctors told me I would never walk, but my mother told me I would, so I believed my mother.

—WILMA RUDOLPH

She knew she had us, and we were everything to her. So she sacrificed, and she worked hard and she made it through.

—HALLE BERRY

Protect and provide for your children from the
beginning until the very end, as if
your life—and theirs—depended on it.

FOUR

Comforter and Friend

As a mother comforts her child,

so will I comfort you.

—Isaiah 66:13

Until the day she died, Mother was my best friend. I found immeasurable comfort in knowing that, even in the midnight hour, I could call her and shewould be there for me,offering advice, sharing a laugh, whispering sweet things to me when I was troubled or confused. Her touch smoothed my ruffled feathers and cooled my feverish forehead.

Black mothers carry within them an instrinsic, unconditional love for their children. It sears through their hearts, straight into our own—and touches everything we touch. It is as sweet as nectar; as pure as God's love itself.

To our mothers who are also our best friends, thank you for being our sturdy bridges. Thank you for so selflessly laying yourselves down for us so that we could cross over to the other side.

—KCT

My mother . . . sturdy black bridge that I crossed over on.

—CAROLYN ROGERS, POET

I am here because of the bridges that I crossed. Sojourner Truth was a bridge. Harriet Tubman was a bridge. Madame C. J. Walker was a bridge. Fannie Lou Hamer was a bridge.

—OPRAH WINFREY

I still hear your humming, Mama. The color of your song calls me home. The color of your words saying, "Let her be. She got a right to be different. She gonna stumble on herself one of these days. Just let the child be." And I be, Mama.

—SONIA SANCHEZ

I was an odd child; I was extremely introverted, very quiet. And my mother would allow that because she was also an introvert; we were kindred spirits.

—GLORIA NAYLOR

There is
no place I'd
rather be tonight,
except in
my mother's arms.

—DUKE ELLINGTON, SPEECH GIVEN
AT THE WHITE HOUSE, 1969

I'm a mama's boy. Always have been . . . The first person we knew was
mama. The first person we kissed was mama. The first person we
shared a laugh with was mama. The first person who has always been
there for us has been mama. The only person who, without hesitation,
would sacrifice personal hopes and dreams for us was mama. Mama
has been a father and a mother, a sister, a brother and a best friend to
us, a person who has always raised us with the care and compassion far
beyond her job description.

—KEVIN CHAPPELL

My mother is my root, my foundation. She planted the seed that I base my life on, and that is the belief that the ability to achieve starts in your mind.

—MICHAEL JORDAN

My mother's was the first hand I ever held; my entire, tiny, newborn hand wrapped around her index finger. I remember seeing that image in a blurred photo one day long ago.

In a very real way, our hands acted out what was happening to our hearts—an inextricable bond and friendship were forming. When you think about it, friendship really does lend itself—quite beautifully—to fingers wrapping, hearts filling, and hands holding. *This* is the stuff of magical, maternal friendship.

—KCT

I did it [raised the children] ad hoc, like any working mother does. Every woman who's got a household knows exactly what I did. I did it on a minute-to-minute basis . . . There was never a place I worked, or a time I worked, that my children did not interrupt me, no matter how trivial—because it was never trivial to them.

—TONI MORRISON

I am most passionate in my relationship with mama. It is with her that I feel loved and sometimes accepted. She is the one person who looks into my heart, sees its needs and tries to satisfy them.

—bell hooks

Mom, you have done so much for me in my life. Here are ten reasons why I like being your child:

1. You are there to comfort me.

2. Our conversations on the way to school make me happy and much less nervous.

3. I love it when you come to my basketball, soccer and baseball games and cheer, advise and comfort me when I am frustrated.

4. I like it when we take trips together and have long chats.

5. I love it when we drink hot chocolate together and talk about personal things that sometimes worry me.

6. It comforts me when you kiss me goodnight.

7. I love seeing you standing there waiting for me as soon as I get off the school bus whether it's rain, sunshine, sleet, hail, lightning or even thunder. It's wonderful to see you standing in the driveway waiting for me.

8. I like it when you take time away from your busy schedule to play basketball with me.

9. I appreciate it when you come to my school whenever I need you.

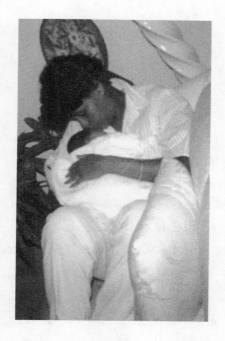

10. I love it when you feel my forehead and hug me when I am sick.

All these things and more are what make my day worth it—always knowing you will be there.

—LONNIE PAUL TAYLOR II,
SON OF KRISTIN CLARK TAYLOR

Girl, my mother can really burn. My grandmother and godmother could also cook, but nobody makes macaroni and cheese like my mama. Now, my godmother used to make it the "easy" way. She'd just put the cooked macaroni in a baking pan, cut up a li'l cheese on top, and splash in some milk. It always came out kind of dry and hard on top, and *that* kind of macaroni and cheese I never liked.

When my mother taught me to make it, my whole attitude about this Sunday dinner staple changed overnight. My mom is the queen of macaroni and cheese—Myra Lou's way may take longer, but baby, it's worth it. She slowly melts the cheese and butter together with the milk and seasonings (she usually adds a beaten egg, I sometimes leave that out). She pours the liquid mixture over the macaroni and adds more cheese cubes. Then she tops it off with cheese slices. It tastes wonderful and is luscious to eat (sorry—not low-cal).

Today, I can make macaroni and cheese just like my mother. And I'm proud of it! Clearly, my mother prevailed over my godmother in this area.

—PHYLLIS ARMSTRONG

MYRA LOU'S
"NO-FAIL" MACARONI AND CHEESE

16 ounces of elbow macaroni or penne (we now use Italian-style penne noodles)

4 cups of milk (canned or whole)

20 ounces of pasteurized American cheese

1/2 stick of butter

1 beaten egg (optional)

1/4 teaspoon salt

1/2 teaspoon white pepper or paprika

8 ounces of cheddar

1/4 cup bread crumbs (optional)

Boil water with a pinch of salt. Add macaroni and cook until just done (baking will soften macaroni more). Rinse with cold water, drain, and pour in large, deep baking dish (a straight-sided soufflé-type baking dish works well). Should be about two-thirds full so you have enough room for the sauce.

Heat milk in medium-size, nonstick saucepan. Cut 16 ounces of American cheese into chunks. Add to milk with butter and melt over low heat. Stir frequently until all the cheese is melted. Add beaten egg if you want a more custard texture to the sauce.

Add seasonings and pour over macaroni. (You may have a little sauce left over. If there's not enough, use more milk next time.)

Cut up 6 ounces of the cheddar into chunks and push down into the macaroni, distributing throughout the dish. Slice remaining 2 ounces of cheddar and 4 ounces of American cheese. Place on top of casserole. Sprinkle on bread crumbs or a little paprika, if you like.

Bake 30 to 40 minutes in a 350° oven or until top is lightly browned and most of the sauce is absorbed. Cool 10 to 15 minutes before serving.

My mother wanted us to look out the window . . . and to see that the world was a big place with lots of opportunities. She wanted to expose us to the open doors that were out there first.

—QUEEN LATIFAH

Yes, Mother . . . I can see that you are flawed. You have not hidden it. That is your greatest gift to me.

—ALICE WALKER

She is free and she is my mother.

—GALATIANS 4:26

MOTHER MAPS

For the last three years, I have set myself a Mother's Day task: to write down all the advice my mother has given me over the course of the year. On the second Sunday in May, after our official Mother's Day celebration has ended, I turn off my phone, turn on my computer and list all the pearls of wisdom, the precious life lessons, my mother, like generations of Black mothers, grandmothers and "othermothers"—the countless Sisters to whom Black daughters are related, not by blood or birth, but by unbreakable bonds—seems to know innately, intuitively, instinctively.

I started this list for two reasons. I thought that if I took the time to put my mother's advice on paper, then maybe all her wisdom, her seventysomething years of world experience, would somehow seep into my brain. Once that happened, I reasoned, I'd be on Easy Street. Life would be a breeze. All that knowledge would make me, if not invincible, at the very least incisive. There'd be no situation I couldn't handle, no problem I couldn't solve, no disappointment I couldn't deal with. (It hasn't happened yet but, hey, you never know; that biological, Black-mother-wisdom thing may kick in at any moment.)

The other reason I started the list, though, is far more important. It's my way of saving my mother's priceless gems of wisdom, of safe-guarding the words that, for my sister and me, made stepping into the unknown possible and dealing with the uncontrollable bearable.

Though I didn't know it when I started them, my Mother's Day lists have become something sacred, something spiritual, something sacrosanct. That's because these lists have become a way to link the future and the past. A way to let the next generation listen to my mother's life. A way of preserving her hard-won experience not just for myself, but forever. I cannot read or write one without remembering so many of the essential truths my mother has made clear to me that no Black woman should ever forget.

For a long time, I didn't know what to call these annual lists. And this year, it finally hit me. The perfect name: Mother Maps. When you think about it, that's what they are. Blueprints to help daughters understand where the trapdoors lie. Beacons for us to follow when we're feeling lost and life's everyday burdens seem too heavy a load.

This year's list contains some real gems, including:

- Failure is not falling down, but staying down.
- Whenever a task looks impossible, remember the old African proverb: When spiderwebs unite they can tie up a lion.
- Always prefer a loss to a dishonest gain; the one brings pain at the moment, the other for all time.
- You are not what people call you; you are what you respond to.
- If you always do what you've always done, you'll always get what you've always got.
- You are the shero of your own story.

"A hard head makes a soft behind." That's what my mother always says when I've disregarded some life lesson she's drilled into me since I was a child and am suffering the consequences.

"Thanks for the sympathy," I moan, trying in vain to win a little bit of hers. "Give me a break; with all the stuff you've told me, you can't seriously expect me to remember *everything*."

Deep down, my mother knows this is not a cop-out. You'd have to have a photographic memory and a genius IQ to retain every single piece of her advice. Vast and varied, it covers everything from trials to triumphs, all things emotional, spiritual, social and familial. But I

think I understand why, when it comes to teaching her daughters how to live in this world, my mother, like African American mothers everywhere, has tried to leave no stone unturned. It's because of our unique history.

"... today's Black mothers' ... racial memory includes African men, women and children being torn from their land and shipped like cargo into slavery in the interest of White men's greed," Johnetta B. Cole, the renowned teacher and Spelman College president emerita eloquently explains it. "In the New World, children were literally taken from their mothers' arms in one of the most cruel systems devised in the West."

And so, for African American mothers, all that advice they give comes down to this: wanting their daughters to know, as Dr. Cole puts it, "as many of their joys and as few of their pains ... as they grow into both their Blackness and their womanness."

Some words you just remember—even without trying. Like Proverbs 22:6. *Train up a child in the way he should go: and when he is old, he will not depart from it.* As a teenager, whenever I'd done something stupid or silly or scary, my mother would repeat these words over and over. As a woman, I finally understand why.

—LAURA RANDOLPH LANCASTER

It was my mother who actually taught me to love to learn. From an early age, she actually instilled deep within me a thirst for knowledge and a quest for excellence. Even though she was balancing—with skill and grace, I must add—the task of raising eleven children by herself, she touched each one of us with her light and she changed our little worlds. She was my mother and my father. My best friend and my confidante. She still is. Would I be where I am today without my mother's wisdom, her fortitude and her strong, unwavering shoulder? Of course not! Am I singing praise to my mother for her selfless courage, her blinding determination, and her steady sense of purpose? Am I thanking her for her gentle heart and her firm hand?

You bet I am. With all my heart. I love you, Ma. You are an angel among us.

—LONNIE P. TAYLOR

Now that we're older, Lonnie Paul isn't as gentle with me as he used to be when I was a baby. I think I can still remember him holding me and rocking me when I was a baby. When I see old photos and family movies, it helps me remember that both Mommy and Daddy wanted us to be brother and sister—but also friends. They want us to know that our whole family is much more than just a family. We're friends, too.

—MARY ELIZABETH TAYLOR,
DAUGHTER OF KRISTIN CLARK TAYLOR

I cannot forget my mother. Though not as sturdy as others, she was my bridge. When I needed to get across, she steadied herself long enough for me to run across safely.

—RENITA WEEMS

Our African American mothers are the sturdy, stone bridges in our lives; strong and unwavering. Be a bridge to your child and actively help him cross to the other side— wherever that "other side" may be.

FIVE
Wise Teacher

She speaks with wisdom,

and faithful instruction is on her tongue.

—Proverbs 31:26

During her spring break from college, Mother gave birth to me, her seventh child. As Mother pursued her education, Daddy and all of my siblings helped nurture me and brought much love and warmth into my young life. To my mom, the pursuit of higher education was one of life's most important goals—for her and for her children—and she kept all seven of us close around her as she persevered through undergraduate school.

My parents were creative: Daddy carried downstairs a cedar dresser drawer from our attic and placed it in the corner of our living room, close to where Mother studied. He lined the drawer with soft, warm blankets and placed me gently into my newly converted "drawer-bed" so that I could be close to her while she studied. I must have enjoyed it: Even now the smell of cedar instinctively warms my heart and comforts my soul.

Mother continued her education and received her master's degree in education when I was two years old. Several journalists and photographers came to our home to take pictures of this incredible woman who was filled with such love and such boundless determination. I sat on my sister's lap for one of the photos, smiling into the photographer's camera, surrounded by my six siblings in our living room. Mother wore her graduation cap for many of the photos.

Even though I was only two, I can somehow still remember the sound of her old Underwood typewriter—tap, tap, tap, tap, space, space, *ding*—as she wrote her master's thesis. By then I'd outgrown the cedar drawer, so I napped in a huge laundry basket under the table where she wrote. It is no coincidence that, between us all, we have twenty-three degrees in our family. It is no coincidence that I nudge my own children toward excellence in education. I know in my heart that my efforts, and my mother's efforts, are—completely and totally—by God's design.

—KCT

Wisdom is the principal thing; therefore get wisdom:
and with all thy getting get understanding.

—PROVERBS 4:7

Oh, Mama was a smart woman. It takes a smart woman to fall in love
with a good man.

—BESSIE DELANEY

I have found . . . thoughts and words to be the foundation for success
and failure in life. I'm teaching my kids when to whisper and when to
shout.

—DIANA ROSS

Jimmy nodded in the same way he did when Mother took him forcibly by the hand to the Museum of Modern Art in New York and made him look. Jimmy didn't mind art if he could see it alone and decided for himself what he liked and what he didn't. But when it came to art, his mother was like his teachers. The questions she responded to were her own, not Jimmy's. And the more she lectured about Picasso and Braque and Cezanne, the more the canvases on the wall began to remind him of math problems on Mrs. Minnafy's blackboard.

—ANNE BEAL, LINDA VILLAROSA,
AND ALLISON ABNER

Neither a lofty degree of intelligence nor imagination nor both together go to the making of a genius. Love, love, love, that is the soul of genius.

—WOLFGANG AMADEUS MOZART

Children are born without ideas about race . . . That means it's up to us as parents to teach them a number of important lessons about race: That all people are equal and no one should be judged by the color of her or his skin. That, unfortunately, racism exists . . . That some of the many achievements of African-Americans and some of our painful history has been left out of the history books. And, most important, that—racism and history aside—your child is a special person who must learn to love her or his beautiful, black self . . . Here are a few ways you can help them develop a good self-image:

- Let them know they're beautiful . . . Statements that show preference for one color or hair texture over another can have devastating consequences for a child.

- Give them brown dolls . . . By giving (or making) your child a doll that looks like him, he will see his hair texture and his eye and skin color as "normal" rather than different or "other."

- Provide them with a safe and loving environment . . . [Dr. Daniel believes] this will not only help your child feel secure and strong in general, but will also provide her with powerful role models in the face of future stereotypes that portray blacks as criminals or negligent parents.

—ANNE BEAL, LINDA VILLAROSA,
AND ALLISON ABNER

Mothers: As you go about the task of molding and teaching your children, let them know that the *quest* for knowledge is abstract and never-ending but that the *attainment* of knowledge, in and of itself, is absolute and certain. Teach them the distinction; and teach them that both paths are right.

—KCT

My mother has always been a constant reader; I can't remember her without a book in her hand, or her travel bag, on the table or—if nowhere in sight—on her mind! That mental picture has turned out to be worth a thousand words—or books, to be precise. When my brothers and I went to help her declutter the basement, we were overwhelmed by the number of paperback books we found . . . My bond with books goes way back, my mother tells me. She named me "Shireen," inspired by what she thought was a beautiful name of a character in one of those paperback novels. What a lasting gift from a reading mother to a loved daughter.

—SHIREEN DODSON

No amount of experimentation can ever prove me right; a single experiment can prove me wrong.

—ALBERT EINSTEIN

My grandmother, Martha Ann Greatheart, could not read or write. But she was a good listener. And she could tell us stories that I suppose other people had to read. Back in my high school days, there were lessons that we could not find in books. My grandmother could tell us exactly when and where historical events occurred. Most of the time, my brother and I would be the only two people in the class who knew the right answers. Because of the fireside stories she told us—full of history, full of folklore about our ancestors, full of wisdom and truth—we became wise, too. By sitting with my grandmother and talking with her near the fire, she was passing on something to us that would remain with her forever: her wisdom.

That's what black mothers should be doing with their children: passing on the old knowledge in any way they can. Like I said, my grandmother didn't know how to read. But she was the wisest woman I ever knew.

—MAGDALENE STURGES TAYLOR,
MOTHER-IN-LAW OF KRISTIN CLARK TAYLOR

In all my efforts to read, my mother shared fully my ambition
and sympathized with me in every way she could. If I have
done anything in life worth attention, I feel sure
I inherited the disposition from my mother.

—BOOKER T. WASHINGTON

My mother, Corine Sturges, who was born in the early 1900s, used to always tell us, "Prepare for war in a time of peace," meaning don't wait until you need something to start making preparations. That was one of her mottos that I follow to this day. If the teacher assigned me two pages of work, my mother would have me read four—always one step ahead . . . My parents always made sure that we attended school daily; through rain, sleet and snow we had to go.

My parents said to us constantly, "You must get an education because you're going to need it one day." Now I find myself repeating

the same words to every child I have a chance to talk to. All four of us graduated from high school. My brother and I graduated together. My parents were so very proud of us because we were the first to graduate from high school on my mother's side of the family; the second on my father's side.

I graduated from high school second in my class, when I was fifteen years old. I attended college at sixteen. Our high school motto when we graduated was: "We have crossed the river, but the ocean lies before us."

How very, very true.

—MAGDALENE STURGES TAYLOR,
IN A PASSAGE FROM THE WRITTEN
HISTORY OF HER FAMILY

When my children were young, I was often an indignant mother. I was indignant with people who tried to hold my children back. I was indignant as I went to their school to ask some white, bourgeois teacher *not to limit my children's potential* just because we were on welfare. Mine were the only three little black children in the school, and no, my children were not treated equally. I had to fight for their education. I remember one of my daughter's teachers once asked why she was reading Shakespeare. She came home and asked me, "My teacher wants to know where we got the money to buy this full, unedited version of Shakespeare's plays." I told my daughter that that was none of the teacher's business—but later on I snuck into the school and very firmly asked that teacher *not* to limit my children's potential, and that if she was gearing them up to work on some assembly line, she was sadly, sadly mistaken because they can *choose* to work on the assembly line—or they can choose to become Lee Iacocca or Henry Ford. My children needed to know that they had options—and I demanded that their teachers realize that as well.

—PAULA WHARTON-LITT

My mother had very little formal education, yet she recognized how incredibly important education was and she constantly hammered on that theme. She felt that even though our lot in life was not very good, we had total control over it through education. She saw education and knowledge as the great equalizer. She used to tell me that it really didn't matter whether anyone else had ever done what I was about to do or not. What I had to keep in focus, she said, was that *I* could do it. I could get all As! I, alone, could move my grades from "Es to As". That kind of confidence, over the course of time, does tend to make you believe you can do anything. When I look back on the whole thing, I don't know that my brother and I were any smarter than anybody else. But with my mother's help, we began to realize that advancement was ours, through education. The power of the human mind and its ability to absorb and retain information is incredible. The power of positive thinking—the power of instilling a positive image and learning all that you possibly can—is crucial. And this applies not only to children but to adults.

I had a very difficult time in school as a child. When my mother saw that I was failing just about everything in school, she said, "I'm sorry, but things have got to change. You can't keep on like this. You cannot spend your time playing outside and watching TV and bringing home grades like this, because you are going to destroy your life. I know you're not going to like this, but no more TV. You can watch only two or three programs during the week. And you've got to not only do your homework but read two books a week, then give me a book report."

Now of course I thought that was a horrible, horrible thing.

Everybody else was out playing and having fun. My friends used to tell me how strict my mother was and how she never let me have any fun, and I agreed with them. But to my mother, what other people said was totally inconsequential—what my friends said, what I said, or what anybody else said. She knew that this was right. She prayed about it. She asked God to give her the wisdom, and she came up with this plan and was absolutely certain that it was going to work. Interestingly enough, after a few weeks, her plan *did* work. I began to understand that I knew things that nobody else knew yet, and it was because I was *reading*.

Then another vitally important discovery was made: My eyesight was of extraordinarily poor quality. So I got glasses, and all of a sudden I could see the blackboard. All of a sudden I could understand what people had been talking about all this time in class. I went from Es to Ds, and I was really quite thrilled with myself and my progress. But my mother said, "But you haven't *done* anything. An E is just as bad as a D because I know you can do so much better than that!" She wouldn't accept anything less than an A. A lot of people say, well, that's not good for parents to put so much pressure on a child. It's unhealthy and unproductive. But I think there must have been something, in both my brother and myself, that led her to believe that we were capable of getting As. She believed in us, and made us believe in ourselves.

—BENJAMIN CARSON, M.D.

My mother's name was Doris Murphy Tanner. She was a very unusual person; filled with wisdom. She had a private pilot's license. She was a first in black aviation, and this accomplishment has been immortalized in a permanent exhibit of Black Aviation at the Smithsonian Air and Space Museum in Washington, D.C. She was a collector of wisdom—quips, quotes, poems—and also wrote letters to her children, and she shared that wisdom with me. I have an entire file of different papers, quotes, poems, quips she left me. Words of wisdom she'd saved and written down and preserved. Here are a few she left for me:

A PARENT'S PRAYER

O heavenly Father, make me a better parent. Teach me to understand my children, to listen patiently to what they have to say, and to answer all their questions kindly. Keep me from interrupting them or contradicting them. Make me as courteous to them as I would have them be to me. Forbid that I should ever laugh at their mistakes or resort to shame or ridicule when they displease me. May I never punish them for my own selfish satisfaction or to show my power.

Let me not tempt my child to lie or steal. And guide me, hour by hour, that I may demonstrate by all I say and do that honesty produces happiness.

Reduce, I pray, the meanness in me. And when I am out of sorts, help me, dear Lord, to hold my tongue.

May I ever be mindful that my children are children and I should not expect from them the judgment of adults.

Let me not rob them of the opportunity to wait on themselves and to make decisions.

Bless me with the bigness to grant them all their reasonable requests and the courage to deny them privileges I know will do them harm.

Make me fair, just, and kind. And fit me, O Lord, to be loved and respected and imitated by my children.

Amen.

—NATALIA TANNER, M.D.

Another precious, golden nugget of wisdom from Doris Murphy Tanner, mother of Natalia Tanner:

A CHILD'S TEN COMMANDMENTS
TO PARENTS

1. My hands are small. Please don't expect perfection whenever I make a bed, draw a picture, or throw a ball. My legs are short. Please slow down so that I can keep up with you.

2. My eyes have not seen the world as yours have. Please let me explore safely. Don't restrict me unnecessarily.

3. Housework will always be there. I'm only little for such a short time. Please take time to explain things to me about this wonderful world; and do so willingly.

4. My feelings are tender. Please be sensitive to my needs. Don't nag me all day long. (You wouldn't want to be nagged for your inquisitiveness.) Treat me as you would like to be treated.

5. I am a special gift from God. Please treasure me as God intended you to do, holding me accountable for my actions, giving me guidelines to live by, and disciplining me in a loving manner.

6. I need your encouragement to grow. Please go easy on the criticism; remember, you can criticize the things I do without criticizing me.

7. Please give me the freedom to make decisions concerning myself. Permit me to fail so that I can learn from my mistakes; and someday I'll be prepared to make the kinds of decisions life requires of me.

8. Please don't do things over for me. Somehow, that makes me feel that my efforts didn't quite measure up to your expectations. I know it's hard, but please don't try to compare me with my brother or sister.

9. Please don't be afraid to leave for a weekend together. Kids need vacations from parents. Besides, it's a great way to show us kids that your marriage is very special.

10. Please take me to Sunday school and church regularly, setting a good example for me to follow. I enjoy learning about God.

When they were very young, my children would see me studying at our kitchen table early in the morning. They thought that I'd awakened early—but they never realized that I'd been up through the entire night, studying. For six and a half years I did that, as I was working toward my degree and advanced degrees. I would have to take them to night school with me, to the university, because we could never afford a baby-sitter. I'd have my children right there with me in class, coloring or reading. And when I graduated, they clapped and cheered so loudly! They were so proud! After a while, *I* was going to *their* graduations. They'd bring home awards and ribbons and I'd put them on display at home. The only reason I graduated and framed my degrees was so that my children could see that they didn't have to stay in public housing. They didn't have to be on welfare. Now that their degrees are hanging in my bedroom, I have taken mine down. It is now their time to shine.

—PAULA WHARTON-LITT

When you get into a tight place and everything goes against you, till it seems as though you could not hang on a minute longer, never give up then, for that is just the place and time that the tide will turn.

—HARRIET BEECHER STOWE

I am in awe of my mother's ability to understand what a boy needed to become a man. Yet most people fail to celebrate the virtues of many black mothers who over the years have functioned—even thrived—in the dual roles of mother and father.

—KWEISI MFUME

Treat the world well . . . It was not given to you by your parents . . . It was willed to you by your children.

—KENYAN PROVERB

I think it's been a combination of my father's and my mother's personalities that has allowed me to become the person that I am. They are so different in some ways yet they are so similar . . . My mother knows how to play the game. That's where I learned how to mingle with CEOs and at the same time still have a good relationship with inner-city kids. That's the game of life; being flexible and open enough to move between different circles of people. My mother has always been more of the business side of the family. She had a kind of "Get up and go get it" attitude . . . She would say, "I think you should get more money, son. I think you should hold out and get what you're worth." That's the business side of my mother. And I have some of that, too.

—MICHAEL JORDAN

A mother is not to be compared with another person.
She is incomparable.

—AFRICAN PROVERB

My mother and grandmother and other mothers and grandmothers raised money, but still not enough to spare us from having to use secondhand, often outdated textbooks from the white schools—books that never included black history. But these women and our teachers . . . supplied something else that money couldn't buy and the law couldn't limit, and that was a sense of pride in who we were and where we came from and where we were going.

—CHARLAYNE HUNTER-GAULT

I find, by close observation, that the mothers are the levers which move in education. The men talk about it . . . but the women work most for it.

—FRANCES WATKINS HARPER,
FOUNDING MEMBER OF NAACP

I've always cherished this photograph of the Bing sisters, the first
family members on my father's side to attend college. In my youth,
being able to talk with these extraordinary, intelligent women about
college was a real-life inspiration to me. I didn't even really know
what college was, but it sure sounded like a wonderful thing. Not only
were they beautiful ladies . . . they were well-educated too!

—MAGDALENE STURGES TAYLOR

Recently, I told my little grandson, Tanner, that if he wanted me to subsidize his skiing lessons this year, we had to have a "contract." One of the terms of the contract was that he had to read a book every week, and give a book report to me. And then I cited that this is the way the mother of Dr. Benjamin Carson (a pediatric neurosurgeon) turned him around. Children need that extra push in their lives.

—NATALIA TANNER, M.D.

Everybody loves a fool, but nobody wants him for a son.

—WEST AFRICAN PROVERB

I had already found that motherhood was a profession by itself: just like school teaching and lecturing.

—IDA B. WELLS

Mother imprinted in my mind a Top Ten list of the wisest things she could share with me. Here is her list, with a slightly updated, modernized version of my own beside it. Interestingly, both lists are timeless.

TOP TEN THINGS A BLACK MOTHER CAN TEACH HER DAUGHTER

Mother's List

Love God constantly.

Never leave the house wearing tattered underwear.

Put a few pennies away for a rainy day.

Stand out beautifully in a room.

Keep your figure, especially after having a baby.

Know that others will judge you by your skin color *first*; all other qualities afterward.

Kristin's List

Love God constantly.

Treat yourself to new underwear once a month.

Set up an IRA.

Learn to work a room deftly; with skill and grace.

Join a health club. *Work that body* to tighten things up and lose those extra baby pounds.

Know that others will judge you by your skin color *first*; all other qualities afterward.

Mother's List

Walk away from trouble.

Know how to throw a good party for your friends and family.

When dining out, don't ever become a member of the "Clean Plate Club."

Black is beautiful.

Kristin's List

Master the art of conflict resolution.

Know how to throw a good party for your friends and family.

Leave a few morsels on your plate so people won't think your mama doesn't feed you.

Black is beautiful..

Our children's minds are like small, absorbent sponges. Lord: Guide us so that we may fill their "sponges" with the thirst to learn. Teach us to teach them to open their eyes to all things wonderful, large and small.

SIX

Loving Surrogate

Biology is the least of what makes

someone a mother.

—Oprah Winfrey

The very notion of large extended black families caring for one another and the existence of "other mothers" throughout our bloodline is deeply rooted in our culture, tradition, and history.

As a child, my other mothers included all of the black women on my block who sat on their porches and kept a loving, protective eye on all the neighborhood children, lest harm come to us as we romped and whooped in the dwindling light of day. They included every one of my six older sisters, who showered me with a sisterly/maternal love as thick as honey while our mother struggled to balance college classes, a full-time job, raising seven children, and maintaining a strong, stable marriage with Daddy.

My other mothers included my grandmother Mama Lilly, who used to whip me up two fried eggs and bacon for breakfast whenever I spent the night and allowed me to eat dinner with her in her living room, from our TV tables, watching *Gunsmoke* and *The Ed Sullivan Show*. They were the ladies in my church who fanned and hummed and nudged me if I squirmed; they were my aunts and great-aunts who used to pull me close and say, "Give Mama some sugar"—even though my own mama was standing right beside me, smiling down on my pigtails and red plaid jumper with love and pride.

Don't we all warmly remember the strong, self-sacrificing African American women who treated us as though we were their own; who filled the role of mother for us—if not for a brief moment, then over the course of a lifetime?

Today we celebrate all of our surrogate mothers; all of the grandmothers who took in their grandchildren when times were incredibly tough; all of the ladies who sat on their porches and, instinctively and protectively, enshrouded us with their love as we played in the evening sunset. To all of the black foster mothers and adoptive mothers, we thank you for helping us realize that bloodlines and gene pools have nothing to do with the ability to love a child unconditionally.

One of the most extraordinary African American mothers I know is my mother-in-law, Magdalene Sturges Taylor, whose maternal love stretches for miles into a boundless sky. In addition to raising eleven healthy, successful children of her own—*alone* (her husband died when her youngest child was six)—she has brought scores of foster children into her home. When my own mother died, the image of Magdalene Taylor as mother and lover of children—in my own eyes—was magnified tenfold, and I clung to her hungrily, desperately, in an effort to fill the void that my mother's death created. She is a tall, strong woman with beautiful, high cheekbones and the most perceptive eyes I've ever seen. Since my mother passed away, she's been my surrogate mother, and I know that I am blessed to have been placed in her path.

Some years ago, this mother, grandmother, and great-grand-mother adopted three additional children who are the same age as my own. In the courtroom during the adoption proceeding, news cameras whirred and journalists took note of this incredible woman who now has fourteen children. In the courtroom on that day, people broke into applause. On that day, souls were warmed. Hearts were uplifted. Lives were changed. Her three new daughters had just begun a wonderful new journey, toward family, love, and the spirit of inclusion. Mrs. Magdalene Taylor is an angel with a "gift" that touches every life around her; rare in her heightened spirituality, extraordinarily wise and intuitive, regal as an African queen, with a heart that warms the world.

—KCT

I believe that every child should be raised in a family. That was the reason I decided to keep my three foster girls together—because if I didn't, they were going to be separated and placed into different homes. My three "newest" children are biological sisters—a set of twins and a sister a year younger. I thought that they should be kept together and placed into the hands of a warm and loving family. *My* family. My girls most definitely feel they are part of our family; they're always bragging at school about all of their "sisters and brothers." They think of us as their real family, which is exactly how we think of them. There are no lines of separation.

When I first got the girls, I received them as foster children and kept them for about three years. The twins were about three and a half years old then, the youngest sister two and a half. I guess you could say what I have is a spiritual "gift." I've always loved children and have spent my lifetime around them. After my eleven children were grown and all finished with high school and went on to higher education, I thought to myself, well, they did good for themselves. It was then that I also began to realize that maybe I *did* have something to offer another child, if nothing but a home and love. So that's what I decided to do. From that day on, we have grown together.

To black women considering adopting or fostering a child, I have some advice: If you don't love children, don't adopt a child. If you're not willing to sacrifice and give these children an unconditional, *special* kind of love, don't adopt or even foster children because these kids come to you with many problems . . . And you *must* be patient.

Do a lot of reading and research on children who have been in foster homes and the dynamics of their being transferred from one home to another. Learn all you can about the process—and about the challenges that lie ahead.

After raising eleven of my own biological children—alone—and watching every one of them grow into healthy, successful adults and begin to have families of their own, I began to feel a strong yearning to give a little bit more of myself. I guess you could say what I have is a spiritual "gift" when it comes to raising and nurturing children. That's why I adopted more children.

My three girls are very special. When the twins came into my home as foster children, I knew right away there was something different—something sweet and something kind of sad—about them.

Even when they were still in diapers and couldn't speak, I knew they were communicating—with me and with each other. They would stand in front of the fireplace mantle in my living room and look at all the photos of my children and grandchildren, and they'd just cry, cry, cry. Especially at night, they'd stand there looking at the photos of my children and cry, tears just rolling down their little cheeks.

I asked God to help me figure out what about those pictures made them so sad; I prayed that He would enlighten me and help me make these girls happier. He answered my prayers. After a while, it began to dawn on me that the photos might be reminding them of someone or something from their past. I began thinking that maybe there was another sister or brother that they'd been separated from. I took hold of that notion and continued to watch them carefully. The crying continued, and so did the pain.

Finally, I began to do some research. I called different adoption agencies and the Department of Health and Human Services, and I continued to pray. By now, I was *certain* there was another child in the picture—somewhere, someplace—and that this child was close to their heart. I kept calling all around the city, but nobody seemed to have any answers. Finally, just as I was about to give up, I found the answer myself; there *was* another sibling—a sister a year younger than they were—who'd been placed in an adoption home. Naturally, once I found out, I requested that the girls have a chance to see their sister again; even for a brief visit. At first the people at the home said no. A few days later, however, I received a call from the home. They'd changed their minds: "You can bring the girls to see their sister if you still want to," they said. Well, I'll tell you . . . that first visit was something else. Were they glad to see each other after having been separated? I really couldn't tell, although I watched very closely. The visit lasted about an hour and a half; it was quite a strange visit to witness.

I noticed immediately that the twins didn't embrace or play with their younger sister; they just kind of played *beside* each other, never touching and never really looking directly at each other. One of the attendants at the home told me that Latoria, the youngest one, had been withdrawn and isolated ever since her arrival. Maybe that initial separation was too much for all three of them. Whatever the case, there was something silent and traumatic at work. Even though this happened years ago, I remember this like it was yesterday because it was close to Christmas.

After that visit at the foster home, I really wanted the three sisters to be together—to be with each other—if only for the holidays. And I wanted them to be with my family. So I called them back and asked the administrators if I could take Latoria home for just the holidays. A few days later, I received a call asking whether I'd be interested in taking Latoria *permanently*. The rest is history. And the rest is also, you could say, our future together, as a family.

Latoria came to my home in time for Christmas, and my three new daughters had the Christmas gift of a lifetime—a new family. Today, they're normal, happy girls, facing the same problems that every young person faces. But this time, they have a family—their own family—to lean on and love. And a whole bunch of sisters, brothers, nieces, nephews, cousins—and *definitely* a mother—who'll love them right back.

To become an adoptive mother, you really need to evaluate *yourself*, too, to determine whether you're willing to give up your time and your emotional energy to raising adoptive children.

I've jotted down some of the things that black mothers need to consider as they raise their children—adoptive, foster, or biological. I begin with a simple, two-letter word: "Be." Just *"be."*

Be truthful to yourself.

Be firm.

Be flexible.

Be a good listener.

Be ready to analyze all situations.

Be supportive.

Be knowledgeable about what's happening in your child's life: at home, at school, and in their other surroundings.

Be a detective.

Be encouraging.

Be prayerful.

And—most important of all—*be there* for your children in their time of need.

—MAGDALENE STURGES TAYLOR

My mother, Myra Armstrong, has been the most influential woman in my life. But two other strong black women also provided love and direction in my youth. I think it was a blessing to have my god-mother, Mary Wright, and my grandmother Zeolar Powell involved in my upbringing.

Mary and James Wright (we called him Jimbo) had three daughters of their own, but still made us feel like we were part of their family. I felt they cared for us as much as they would have if they had been our birth parents. Although my mother was still in our lives, the Wrights took on a lot of the caregiving until I was ten years old.

I was just two when my mother and father separated. As a young, single mother, she needed help taking care of her children, so we moved back home to St. Louis. It was my godparents who stepped in and gave me, my brother, and later my sister a stable home environment while my mother worked.

Over the years, the Wrights took a number of children into their home. It was lonely for me sometimes because my godparents were very strict and there weren't any children my age living close enough to be regular playmates. Daydreaming in the backyard alone probably contributed to my active imagination and love of reading. My godparents were Catholic and God was a constant in our lives. We got up every Sunday and went to church. After mass, we'd go home and cook breakfast before starting the Sunday dinner. Everyone had chores assigned to them. We all did our part and shared everything, from household chores to clothes. My godmother had a beauty salon in her basement and I can remember the laughter, work, and conversation that filled the place with a sense of community.

My godparents didn't have a lot of money. They just used their wits and wisdom to take care of their children and those of other parents who were trying to get it together. Another one of my fondest memories has to do with the dinner we had sometimes when Catholics couldn't eat meat on Friday. We'd sit around the table and cook up these big, flat biscuits on a flat grill. The best part was smothering them in butter and syrup. I thought those biscuits were heaven. It wasn't until much later that I learned that the "special treat" was the result of a tight food budget.

It was heart-wrenching for the Wrights to let me go when my mother married James Taylor Yokely and we moved to Denver, Colorado.

The life my grandmother led was an interesting contrast to my godmother's home, and it fueled a healthy competition between the two women. They both used to quiz me about how I spent my time with the other, and I think it was because they both wanted to be important to us. My grandmother lived on Fee Fee Road and she had one of the most beautiful homes in Robertson, Missouri. She'd gotten it by being among the most successful black businesswomen of her time. My grandmother was worldly, well traveled, savvy, and very intelligent. Whenever I went to her house, there was a lot of energy and motion. People from all walks of life would often be around doing business or socializing; from local farmers, ministers, and maids to businessmen, gamblers, and truck drivers. Over the years, she outlived several husbands. She owned a landfill, a restaurant, and a nightclub she named after herself, called Club La Zeolar. My mother worked for her sometimes and I spent the summer helping in the restaurant (and eating the cobbler she made to go with the barbecue dinners).

My grandmother could have written the book on the work ethic. When she had struggled enough and saved enough to buy land and property, she brought her relatives up from the South and gave other people a chance to move North. She made it possible for whole families to make it by putting the parents to work in her businesses and providing affordable housing. If she couldn't provide a job, she usually knew enough people or had enough influence to get them employment somewhere. In fact, you didn't go to Zeolar's house unless you planned to work. She'd feed you and you'd eat good—but not without contributing something. My job was often dusting. She had beautiful French Provincial furniture throughout the house and Chinese chairs and tables with intricately curved legs. I had to get down on my hands and knees to dust them bad boys—and believe me she'd check for fingerprints.

My godmother and grandmother both contributed to the woman my mother became and therefore influenced me directly and through her. Together, these three women gave me a great sense of adventure and a deep respect for independence. They taught me what hard work and determination can accomplish. Consequently, I feel blessed to have crossed over the bridges they built for me on my way to a career in broadcast journalism. My own quest for excellence and desire to do best are a reflection of the love they gave to a little girl with dreams.

—PHYLLIS ARMSTRONG

Love thy neighbor as thyself.

—MATTHEW 19:19

I have six children—four that I gave birth to. I am blessed. We've been through some hard times, but we are very blessed now. I went to a program called For the Love of Children (FLOC) in Washington, D.C., and joined their Hope and a Home program. My husband and I saved our money, and FLOC helped get us on our feet. We joined a home buyers' club, we planned, and we saved. Being so blessed made me want to give back. There was a woman in the program with me who had two daughters. She was very sick. I remember one day I saw her on the street, walking with her daughters. She saw me and said, "Linda, how about taking my girls?" I was shocked. I said to her, "Take your *girls?* What do you mean?" She said, "I'm sick, and I just can't care for them anymore." When I saw her on the street that day, I realized she really *couldn't* care for herself—or her daughters. Her hair hadn't been combed for weeks. She looked very weak. Over the next two years, I kept her girls on and off; and she just got sicker and sicker. They came to me—to stay, this time—three days before she passed on. She had written a will that I take them. By then, they were already a part of my family. I love them like they are my own children. I have six children. And all of them are mine.

—LINDA MYRICK

My aunt who had thirteen children of her own raised three more. She had become a midwife, and a child was born who was covered with sores. Nobody was particularly wanting the child, so she took the child and raised him . . . and another mother didn't want to be bothered with [her] two children. So my aunt took one and raised him . . . they were part of the family.

—ELLA BAKER

I have not borne any female children. And yet, I am a surrogate mother to many daughters, seventeen hundred of whom are students at Spelman College.

—JOHNETTA B. COLE

Everyone loved my mom, and she had become kind of like the team mom: having kids over all the time, letting everybody sleep over when they wanted, cooking everyone all kinds of great food . . . She took care of us *all* and never said boo about it.

—TERRELL DAVIS

Over the course of three decades, I've raised fifty-six children: nieces, nephews, foster children, and my own biological children. I was married at the age of fourteen. I was too young. I had to give my baby up when I was a teenager. Taking care of others as I got older helped ease the guilt and pain of giving my first one up. Every single last one of the children I raised is mine, even though they did not all come through me. As poor as we were, it didn't matter. Because we had so much love. They knew they had God's love. And they knew they had mine.

—SCARLETTE GOODE-HUNLEY

The black woman in the South who raised sons,
grandsons, and nephews had her heartstrings
tied to a hanging noose.

—MAYA ANGELOU

If you can't hold them in your arms,
please hold them in your heart.

—CLARA "MOTHER" HALE

My mother was a wet-nurse, if you know what I mean. So many white
people had babies that didn't have any milk, breast milk. My mother
was just like a little dairy. She would get babies all the time. When I
was a baby, my milk went to the other white kids and I got the
strippings.

—WILLIE MAE FORD SMITH

I am the youngest of fifteen children. My mother died when I was born. I never knew anything about being raised by a mother—but I certainly knew about being "mothered," raised, and nurtured by fourteen wonderful, supportive brothers and sisters. I had the most wonderful childhood. It was like a fairy tale. My brothers and sisters cared for me unconditionally. They never *not* loved me. Not one day. No, my mother wasn't there. But I had fourteen other mothers who loved me more than life itself. I'd also like to share a word of advice to mothers, or to any parent who is separated. To separated parents, I say, "Teach your children to love both their parents." Even after my first husband and I separated, I taught my children to love him more than you can imagine—even when I hated him. They are three happy children to this day because I spared them the bitterness I felt. I didn't allow hatred to have any place in their hearts. They love their dad.

—PAULA WHARTON-LITT

My grandmother gave me the reinforcement and adulation that I didn't get from my mother. I think my grandmother had the inner security that allowed her to look outward that my mother didn't have.

—MICHAEL WEBB

*To our surrogate moms, thank you for your selflessness,
your courage, and your generosity. Thank you for your
willingness to help us grow and blossom, even though we came
to you from soil that was not your own. Thank you for
so gently transplanting us into your lives and for
being there when we needed you most.*

SEVEN

IMAGE OF BEAUTY

The more blackness a woman has,

the more beautiful she is.

—Alex Haley

The sight of my mother—stunning, petite, and perfectly poised—still shines in my eyes as clearly as it did when she was alive. Her physical beauty raced before her; as she entered a room, people would turn to admire her before she could even utter a word. She began college before she got married, and as a way to help pay her tuition, she modeled for several art schools across the country and was dubbed "Brown Venus" by the black media and the fashion world.

When I was a child, Mother filled my eyes with her physical beauty and grace. I'd sometimes "sneak peeks" of her in various moments of repose. From our banister in the hallway, I would crouch and watch as she bent this way and stretched that way to water our philodendrons. From under the kitchen table, I'd sit silent and cross-legged, watching her small, slippered feet move from refrigerator to cupboard to oven.

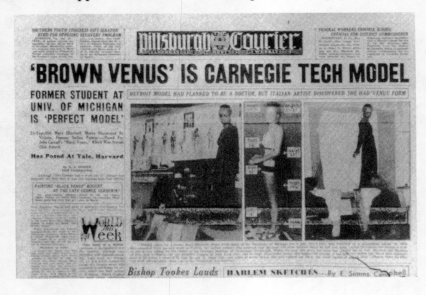

At night, when my siblings were asleep and my father was at work, I'd sneak downstairs to gaze at her sitting at the table in our living room, head bent in concentration, pencil gently tapping the tip of her perfect little mouth, as she created and revised lesson plans for her students.

She was, beyond a doubt, the most beautiful woman I'd ever laid eyes on. And—what's even better—this beautiful, brown woman was my mother. My mother!

Queen of the Nile. Brown Venus.

—KCT

My mother is a beautiful woman who was stunning in her youth. My grandfather was half Native American, and as with many of our people, my family's bloodlines were passed down from more than one race. None of us, however, had any doubt about our black heritage. Although my mother is very fair-skinned, she resented anyone thinking she wasn't black. I can remember people asked if she was Latina or from India or something, and she would be *highly* offended. She would correct them immediately—and with "attitude." There was never any question in her mind about who she was.

I'm always telling people who comment on my complexion that I got my beautiful skin from my mother. I also have her lovely brown eyes, but not nearly enough of her charm. My mom has a radiant personality and enjoys an active life. She has friends younger and older than she is, and many have been close to her for years. When I think about it, I probably learned about making lifelong friends from the example she set. She always taught me you can get more with honey than vinegar. So my tendency toward being kind more often than not, I believe, came from my mother.

—PHYLLIS ARMSTRONG

To describe my mother would be to write about a hurricane in its perfect power.

—MAYA ANGELOU

My mother was a beautiful woman. She had a whole lot of style, with an East Indian, Carmen McRae look and dark, nut brown smooth skin. High cheekbones and Indian-like hair. Big beautiful eyes. Me and my brother Vernon looked like her. She was a very glamorous woman, always dressed to kill. I got my looks from my mother and also my love of clothes and sense of style. I guess you could say I got whatever artistic talent I have from her also.

—MILES DAVIS

Shout my name to the angels
Sing my song to the skies
Anoint my ears with wisdom
Let Beauty fill my eyes

—WALTER DEAN MYERS

No eyes that have seen beauty ever lose their sight.

—JEAN TOOMER

If you walked into a room with my mother, several things would be readily apparent. She would walk into a room, and conversation would stop. She had that kind of presence. She'd enter a room with a smile on her face, kind of laughing, maybe on my stepfather's arm, for example; or with her children at her side. Always a smile and some kind of ongoing, fun mischief that she was encouraging. Her personality entered the room. Women would admire her. Men would admire her. She was about 5′6″, a very shapely woman. She was fair-skinned, with pretty features. I remember she took me to buy my first pair of gabardine pants, which was a real rite of passage for me as a young man. I was twelve going on thirteen. The man fitting me for my pants said to me, "Who's this woman you're with?" "That's my mother," I said. He couldn't believe that this beautiful woman was my mother. The whole time we were in that store, he spent more time looking at my mother, admiring her beauty. I was lucky to leave that day with the right color and right size pants, because that man *definitely* wasn't focusing on me. She handled her beauty with such skill and grace.

—RONNY B. LANCASTER,

ON HIS MOTHER,

JOETTA ELIZABETH TOBIN

Grace was all in her steps,
heav'n in her eye,
In every gesture dignity and love.

—JOHN MILTON

I was so busy checkin' out the brothers as they was checkin' out the sisters that I didn't even realize that one of the sisters being "checked out" was my mama. "Ah, hey now, hey," I said to the fellas who still hadn't realized it was Mama they was whistling at. "Y'all better get your young, narrow butts back down to the [pool] hall cause this woman you're trying to mess with is my *mama*. Mama was decked out, too. She was wearing a pair of nineteens, a white and yellow polka dot hat and a yellow dress that shined like the sun. If any of the brothers had made a move on *my* ma, I'd a had to get with 'em. Lucky for them, none of them made a move. I don't play that with Moms. It's just that she was so fine people didn't know how to act.

—ELLIS THOMPSON, ON HIS MOTHER,
DOROTHY LEE THOMPSON

My mother took me to see Marian Anderson. When I saw this
wonderful woman come from the wings in this white satin dress, I
knew instantly: one of these days, I'm going to come out of the wings.
I don't know what color the dress is going to be but I'm going to be
center stage, right there, where I saw her. The light dawned. It was a
magic moment.

—LEONTYNE PRICE

My mother was a very attractive woman. She had no end to potential suitors, but she always put them on the back burner. She always wanted us to know that my brother and me were the most important things to her, more than anybody else. She made that very clear in all of her actions and all of her words. She was very pretty, but that didn't matter to her. What *did* matter to her was her sons, and our feeling complete. And if that meant her working two or even three jobs at a time, she was going to work two or three jobs at a time. If it meant she had to wear the same clothes all the time, then she'd wear the same clothes all the time if it meant providing clothes for me and my brother. For a young, attractive woman to basically give up on herself and sacrifice so *much* of herself for her children was really a pretty powerful thing.

—BENJAMIN CARSON, M.D.

Take the time to appreciate the intrinsic beauty of the African
American mother in all her grace and splendor. We are
proud, sun-kissed strands of terra-cotta beauty. Begin today to
open your eyes fully to the "Beautiful Ones" in your life,
young and old. Capture their image on film, on canvas, or even with
a simple drawing. Sadly, the small, crucial details we think
we will remember for a lifetime—the twinkle in her eye, the mystery
in her smile, the smoothness of her skin—will dissipate
over time. Capture her beauty permanently, so that it can be
passed on to our children's children.

EIGHT

DISCIPLINARIAN

Train up a child in the way he should go:

and when he is old,

he will not depart from it.

—*Proverbs 22:6*

Mother very rarely laid a hand on any of us, but Daddy could stop us in our tracks with one sidelong glance. Still, both of them created a healthy balance in our household, so there were never any life-threatening "whuppings." Besides, we were too busy being a family, too preoccupied with trying to excel, too totally focused on supporting each other, to concern ourselves with spankings and physical discipline. The seven of us children pretty much kept ourselves in check—because we knew we had to.

Our African American mothers are known for not taking any "foolishness" from their offspring. It is their traditionally firm hand and unflagging rigidity that has kept us on the right track. And for this, black mothers, we praise you and we thank you—even for the "whuppins."

—KCT

I remember how easy it was for my mother to snap me back into line
with a simple rebuke: "I'm ashamed of you. You embarrassed the
family." I would have preferred a beating to hearing those words.
I wonder where our national sense of shame has gone.

—COLIN POWELL

You may be a pain . . . , and you may be bad,
but child, you belong to me.

—RAY CHARLES

I've always believed that children have a built-in "hypocrisy" antenna. If you say one thing and then you do something else, it goes up their antenna and blocks out everything else you're saying. We transmit values, discipline, respect, integrity, through *example*. You clearly have to show you mean what you say, by *doing*. While my mother, for example, was telling us how important education was, she was sitting in her room trying to read a book. We didn't know initially that she might be in there for three hours trying to read one page, but that was what she was doing. She wouldn't just go and prop herself up in front of a TV like so many other parents—at the same time they're telling their kids to go do their homework. She'd be trying to educate herself. She taught us by example. With both my brother and me, she had a very no-nonsense approach. She taught it. And she lived it.

—BENJAMIN CARSON, M.D.

I brought you into this world, child.
And Lord knows I can take you out.

—POPULAR AFRICAN AMERICAN SAYING

What are the eight most frightening words in the English
language when they come from Mama's mouth?
"Go out back and get me a switch!"

—ANONYMOUS

Mother . . . despite her physical delicacy, was a formidable figure when she had a switch in hand.

—JOHNNIE COCHRAN, JR.

When it came to her children, she [my mother] didn't play. She wasn't about to let anyone mess with us. When all else is crumbling is when you have to call up that fighting spirit . . . She was a quiet fighter. The best fighters aren't the big bullies with the muscle but those who just make it happen every day with no fanfare or bravado. They just do what they have to do to survive.

—QUEEN LATIFAH

Always end your child's name with a vowel, so that when you yell, the name will carry.

—BILL COSBY

One late afternoon when I was about five or six years old, I remember my grandfather getting up from the front porch, stretching, and saying something like, "I'm about to go on a walk. Be back in a while. " I wanted to go with him, but he told me I couldn't. I went anyway, and he kept telling me to go back. Well, it turned out the reason he didn't want me to go was because he was going to take a leak. As soon as he got back, he went straight into the house and told my mother. Lord, was she mad. "I'm gonna whip your butt!" she told me—so I scurried under the house. She waited there for me, next to the pillar. After a while it was getting dark, so I *had* to come out. Mama was still standing there waiting. She whipped me until the sun was all the way down. She whipped me for the old and the new. Because of my mother, I came to understand the value of listening to my elders. I found out the hard way that I should have listened to— and obeyed—my grandfather in the first place.

—MAGDALENE STURGES TAYLOR

As I raised my children, I taught them the basic tenets of appropriate human behavior: respect in themselves and others, decency, generosity. But one of the most important things I used to tell them was that it was absolutely vital to do the right thing, even when nobody else was looking over their shoulder. And when they didn't do the right thing, there was hell to pay—but those moments were few and far between. My oldest daughter knew that I needed them to do the right thing, otherwise we'd all sink. I didn't need to impose curfews, and I didn't ground my children. Spankings were never an issue, either, because they knew they had to act like they had some sense. There was no other choice . . . I did used to yell, though. There was lots of noise in our home, but it was loving noise. I just don't believe that anyone should discipline a child unless they can love them equally as much.

—PAULA WHARTON-LITT

He who spares the rod hates his son, but he who loves him
is careful to discipline him.

—PROVERBS 13:24

Being so young herself, and with my father away ministering so much of the time, I think she [my mother] felt she had the right to be a harsh disciplinarian. She never spared the rod. Even when we were too old to spank, Mama was still tough as nails, and we crossed her at our own risk.

—DARLENE LOVE

Because I said so.

—ALL MOTHERS

When my mother commenced to gritting her teeth, pursing her lips,
or narrowing her deep, brown eyes at us, we all knew we'd
better straighten up and "fly right." To our black mothers who kept
us in line, we praise you. Whether it was with the rod or with
your raised eyebrow, you did what you had to do to let
us know that straightening up and flying right
was really the only option we ever had.

NINE

KEEPER OF
THE FLAME

❧

We have a formidable history,

replete with the voice of God, the

ancestors, and the prophets.

—*"The Essential Grounds,"* Afrocentricity

Generational continuity lies at the heart of the black family unit. Elders passing on knowledge, wisdom, folklore, and family history to our younger generations is what keeps our culture colorful, coherent, and crackling with life and vitality. Black mothers are often charged with being the historians of the family; they are the lamplight that leads the way when the pages of our family histories grow dim and are difficult to decipher. Black mothers are the keepers of our family flame, and we must treat our "keepers" with great reverence, care, and respect. Teach your children to learn the right ways to become keepers of the family flame. Teach them to preserve and protect memories, to keep intact the folklore and history of our people, and to work purposefully to keep our legacies alive. Teach them that with age comes wisdom and a powerful sense of familial history that will only stay alive through their deliberate efforts to keep it alive.

—KCT

TRIBUTE TO MY GRANDMOTHER

A cherry tree grew in her front yard bearing fruit in the summer season. When I think of my grandmother, that tree comes to mind for good reason. It was a beautiful and bountiful tree; a perfect haven for a little girl with dreams. I hear my grandmother's voice; soft, yet so commanding: "Chil', don't you eat up all my cherries! Come on out that tree. I got somethin' for you to do." She always did, it seemed.

You see, inside the southern grande dame my grandmother was, beat the heart of a four-star general. She could have led troops into battle, so confident and courageous she was in her ability to teach, lead, and inspire. I can still hear her saying: "Now, get that dust off those table legs! I'll be coming back to inspect your work, you hear?" Dust rag in hand, I tackled the impressive material rewards of my grandmother's enterprising desires.

Her journey through life began in Mississippi, where she was born. She used to enjoy riding to town with her father. But the woman many would later call Chicken had a yearning to fly much farther. Back in the early 1900s, she even traveled to Europe and beyond. No one could convince this incredible black woman that she didn't have wings.

So she flew . . . taking off for New Orleans, where she got married. She eventually left that nest to follow a vision meant for kings. You see, my grandmother was a queen; the royalty of strong, African blood running through her veins. So she flew . . . landing in Missouri with her son to begin hatching her plans from humble beginnings. From elevator operator to office cleaner, she rose, gathering momentum from her successful dealings.

In a time before civil rights and affirmative action, my grandmother forged ahead, refusing to recognize any glass ceilings. She saved her money . . . searched for possibilities . . . bought land . . . and bought property. By the time she married my grandfather she had already turned her ambition into opportunity. The grandmother I came to know when I was less than a decade old lived in the biggest house on Fee Fee Road. But it's what she did for others that demands her story be remembered, cherished, and told.

She brought relatives and friends up from the South . . . gave them jobs and a chance to thrive. She had a landfill in Robertson, a nightclub, and a barbecue restaurant that encouraged others to strive.

I still hear my grandmother pushing, pulling, and prodding others to try. You see, she was a blazing star in the business world long before African Americans were permitted to climb corporate rungs.

Old man McDonnell—as in McDonnell Douglas Aircraft—sure recognized that Zeolar Powell had a powerful song that needed to be sung. His company used her land and his employees ate her barbecue dinners until her "open" sign no longer hung.

I am where I am . . . I am who I am . . . partly because of what my grandmother made of her visionary sight. Everyone she touched . . . everyone she helped . . . everyone she loved, gained from the brilliance of her light.

I will never forget what she taught me long ago: "Don't be afraid of hard work," she advised. "And make sure you do it right."

When I think of my grandmother, I will always remember that anything is possible if you have the will and the courage to take flight.

—PHYLLIS ARMSTRONG'S MEMORIAL TRIBUTE

TO HER GRANDMOTHER

If a house is to be set in order, one cannot begin with
the present; he must begin with the past.

—JOHN HOPE FRANKLIN

Generational continuity is most important among black families; it gives our children a sense of belonging and a sense of what their own contributions will make to the future. Once they can reflect on the traditions that have been passed on through many generations, I think they're more likely to continue them. Some of the happiest times we've had together as a family have been in our house in the country, in Paw Paw, Michigan. This house belonged to my mother's father, and then it was passed on to my mother, and then on to me. We continue to have family gatherings there, on Labor Day, Memorial Day, and the Fourth of July. The house is filled with family pieces that belong to my grandparents and my parents. Everything in the house has been "recycled"—from someplace we have been or from our ancestors. We call our house "Ski and Tee," which are the two major sports we participate in—skiing and golf. My grandson loves it there. He's very free and happy. Skiing has always been a close way of bonding for our family. My children literally grew up on skis. I've continued this multigenerational tradition with my grandson, Tanner Oliver Long. He *loves* it. Another of the traditions we have in our house in the country is the ringing of a school bell when it's time for dinner. This is a handheld bell. I ring it when I want them to come in for dinner. So we have this wonderful bell in Paw Paw. And when I ring it, my family comes.

—NATALIA TANNER, M.D.

The most cherished tradition that I share with my three children—and this is going to sound a little strange—is sleeping on the floor with them when they come home for Christmas. After all these years—and my children are grown now—we all get together in my living room and sleep together on the floor again. It is our time to talk and to remember. To talk about the days when we were on welfare, when times were very tough for us. My children want to reach for the stars—which I've always encouraged—but I also want to keep their feet firmly planted on the ground. So this tradition of getting together and *remembering* is vital to us as a family and to me as a mother. And when we sleep on the floor and talk, we remember this: We had just come to Canada. I was very young then and separated from their father. We knew no one in Canada. We had just gotten on welfare, and we were, in a sense, lost. For the first year or so, we all slept in the same bed in our house in the projects, me and my son and my two daughters. We slept together in one bed because I wanted my children to know that I wasn't going anywhere. And because we were all afraid. Their father had gone, but I was in this for the long haul. They needed me, and I was like a blanket covering them—and I needed them just as much. My children were the reason I stayed alive during that time. This is why our tradition of remembering is so important; because it gives us a chance to look back. My children are grown now—one is a lawyer, one is a doctor, and one is finishing a master's in physical therapy. They all have good, fancy jobs. But we never forget to remember.

—PAULA WHARTON-LITT

I am not ashamed of my grandparents for having been slaves. I am only ashamed of myself for having at one time been ashamed.

—RALPH ELLISON

It is painful to me, in many ways, to recall the dreary years I passed in bondage. I would gladly forget them if I could. Yet the introspection is not altogether without solace; for with those gloomy recollections come tender memories of my good old grandmother, like light, fleecy clouds floating over a dark and troubled sea.

—HARRIET JACOBS, SLAVE

I have two grandchildren. My father passed about five years ago. The saddest part about it is that we never knew anything about my father's family. My siblings and I—and there are thirteen of us—we never knew my father's people. He told us he ran away from home when he was thirteen and never went back. Before he died, he asked us to help him search for his mama; she was somewhere in Alabama, that much he knew. We did the best we could to find her, but we just couldn't. I didn't realize at that time how important it was. I want to know how my grandmother looked. I want to know if I have aunts and uncles. All we know is that she was somewhere in Tuskegee, Alabama. When I look at my children and grandchildren—three generations still alive in our family—I realize how important family memories are. I get sad when I think about the family I never knew that was my father's. It makes my own family even more important. We get together all the time. Three generations. I cook a big Thanksgiving dinner every year, and we always see each other. I only wish I had more to hold on to from my father's side. Now I'll never know.

—LINDA MYRICK

My life flows from you mama. My style comes from a long line of Louises who picked me up in the night to keep me from wetting the bed. A long line of Sarahs who fed me and my sister and fourteen other children from watery soups and beans and a lot of imagination. A long line of Lizzies who made me understand love. A long line of black people holding each other up against silence.

—SONIA SANCHEZ

My mother lives with us, so I have the opportunity and the blessing of seeing her influence on my own son. I also feel a tremendous amount of satisfaction from being able to see her, finally, live her elderly years in comfort. She can go wherever she wants. She's still spry. She loves to garden, and there's lots of flowers on our property. She gets to travel throughout the country and other countries—things she never even dreamed of being able to do. After all of our struggles during my youth, it's wonderful for me to be a witness to her joy and fulfillment today. The other thing that pleases me so is that my mother is able to influence my son, in the same way she influenced me. That same kind of you-can-do-anything, no-excuse-making, hold-your-feet-to-the-fire strive for excellence is being passed right down to my son, by my mother. She just has a gift for that. And for making people feel capable. People who discard their parents are making a grave mistake. They miss the intergenerational wisdom. And that wisdom should never be taken for granted or ignored. If anything, it must be preserved and passed along.

—BENJAMIN CARSON, M.D.

Mama loved black authors. She not only liked what they wrote, but she loved what they represented: history; the preservation of black culture; the keepers of the flame. She saw black writers as creative channels who could reach over, through and into future generations. Their written words, she used to say, would live on forever. Mama was definitely what you'd call a keeper of the flame—our family flame. Her favorite quote was this: "Know from whence you came. If you know whence you came, there is really no limit to where you can go."

—ANN WILSON

On and on my mother would go. No small part of my life was so unimportant that she hadn't made note of it, and now she would tell it to me over and over again.

—JAMAICA KINCAID

Your power is in your faith. Keep it and pass it on to other bloods.

—ARTHUR LEE SMITH, PH.D.

We are African women and we know, in our blood's telling, the tenderness with which our foremothers held each other.

—AUDRE LORDE

Role model? My mother leads the pack.
I regard her as I do all of the other black women
throughout history. Miraculous.

—CICELY TYSON

Black mothers are indeed the keeper of the flame, and we are all responsible for keeping that flame burning. When generations die off, there are ways to bridge the gap. My daughter has come to know her grandmother solely through her memories. My family and I have something we call Grandma Jodi Day [after Mama]. Every November 17, which is my mother's birthday, many of my family members will send my daughter cards and gifts to celebrate Grandma Jodi Day. And what we all tell her is this: "If Mama had lived for you to meet her, she would have spoiled you to no end. She would have showered you with gifts and love." It's so important to create and invent ways to celebrate the richness we all have in our heritage that has been given so generously to us by our ancestors, by our mothers. Try to make it as concrete as possible. This is the way we try to make it real for my daughter.

—RONNY B. LANCASTER

I am a product of every other black woman before me who has done or said anything worthwhile. Recognizing that I am part of that history is what allows me to soar.

—OPRAH WINFREY

I absorbed from [my mother] lifelong habits of hard work and self-discipline. She had never stopped working until she was incapacitated . . . I never understood how she could work so hard from home every day, yet never allow my sister or me to feel anything but mothered. Parents are a luck of the draw. With my mother and father, I could not have been luckier.

—COLIN POWELL

My grandmother was the keeper of our family flame. What she left me when she passed was her *strength*. She left me with the sound belief that whatever you set out to do, you can do it. She was a strong, proud black woman in her neighborhood. *Everybody* respected her. She had raised twelve children, and raised them well. I know it was her flame that I drew upon to find the strength to raise my own eleven children when my husband died. If she did it, then I knew I could do it. With the help of the Lord, I *knew* I could make it. There was never any doubt in my mind. Times got really tough there sometimes. But there was never any doubt in my mind that we would survive as a family. That is what I hope I've passed on to my own children, and they're passing on to theirs. The idea that all things are possible with the help of the Lord. And the idea of an inner strength that cannot be suppressed by anyone or anything. My grandmother lived until she was 102 years old. If that's not an eternal flame, then I don't know what is. Now my father's mother lived near Barnwell, South Carolina. I remember as a child, we would visit her on Saturdays or Sundays after church. She grew banana trees. I thought that was a great thing, to grow banana trees. No one else around had banana trees. She said that she was going to give me one when I was old enough to take care of it. She never did. She was always coming and going from different people's home throughout the county. She was the midwife for that part of the county.

—MAGDALENE STURGES TAYLOR

When times get tough, rejoice in the knowledge
that you are one in a long line of proud, courageous people
who have a history of surviving.

—DENISE STINSON

I always ask you, Mommy, why did you name me Mary Elizabeth?
Because Jesus' mother's name was Mary? And you always say "yes,
sweetie"; it's because of that and it's because the name "Mary" has
been passed down in our family for four generations. That's the part
I *really* like to hear—the part about the generations—even though I've
heard you say it a hundred times before and I already know the
answer. I really like that my name is Mary. It helps me know that I
am an important part of my family's history.

—MARY ELIZABETH TAYLOR

*Teach your children to preserve, appreciate, and pass on
their legacy. Encourage them to cherish things rare; to learn
the technical ways to preserve old family documents,
photographs, antiques. And when it's finally their turn
to pass the familial torch, we want it to shine and
shimmer as brightly as the noonday sun.*

TEN

Ode to Black Mothers

❧

Weep not; she is not dead,

but sleepeth.

—Luke 8:52

When a mother dies, the grief is paralyzing. It can stop us in our tracks; sometimes we even pray for it to stop our hearts. The black cloak of death is immobilizing and shocking in its intensity. It is extremely rude—brutish, even. It snatches all of our sensibilities away without even the slightest apology or warning.

But—fortunately, and over time—some of what is snatched from us is retrievable. Fortunately, there is such a thing as growth through grief. Like the small, green buds that push their way through the gray, cracked earth after a forest fire, life does continue. It has taken me years to realize this. And now I'll spend the rest of my life being grateful for having uncovered the knowledge that joy, as it says in the book of Psalms, *does* come in the morning.

—KCT

By medicine life may be prolong'd, yet death
Will seize the doctor too.

—WILLIAM SHAKESPEARE

I am not going to die,
I'm going home like a shooting star.

—SOJOURNER TRUTH

I have glorified thee on the earth; I have finished the
work which thou gavest me to do.

—JOHN 17:4

I can remember when I was a little girl, how my old mammy would sit out of doors in the evenings and look up at the stars and groan, and I would say, "Mammy, what makes you groan so?" And she would say, "I am groaning to think of my poor children; they do not know where I be and I don't know where they be. I look up at the stars and they look up at the stars."

—SOJOURNER TRUTH

My mother died a hard death . . . Maud "Arie" Powell died on June 3, 1984. The week before, knowing the end was near, I had driven the whole family to New York for what I sensed might be the last visit. It touched me, the closeness that bound my wife and all three children to my mother. The kids all called her "darling," a pleasing sound they had picked up because that was what she called them.

—COLIN POWELL

You died when I was six, Mama . . . Because you died without warning, Mama, my sister and I moved from family to stepmother to friend of the family. I never felt your warmth again.

—SONIA SANCHEZ

I don't recall much at all about the days or nights following my mother's death. Even though I had held her as she took her last breath, I was unwilling to believe Mama had actually left me forever. The thought of seeing her in a casket, eyes closed eternally, was too much for me to bear . . . The thought of being left alone in the world without Mama frightened me. The fact that I had no choice would make me survive.

—KWEISI MFUME

Sometimes I feel
Like a motherless child,
Sometimes I feel
Like a motherless child,
A long way from home,
A long way from home.

—NEGRO SPIRITUAL

I am astonished by her, the good mother. She has called me to her sickbed, not so much to help her as to help *me*. I, in childhood, was never hungry, never homeless, never seriously ill; and was never exposed to the sight of physical suffering. My parents had made sure of all that. But an easy ride of a life is only a half-truth. Now Mama's gift is to let me know her pain. She is letting me see if I am strong enough to grapple, by proxy, with Death.

—LOIS F. LYLES

My mother died when she was in labor with me. I remember when I was just a toddler, people would come to the house and say, "Oh, *you're* the last one?" They'd say to me, *"You're* the one who killed Edna?" (I was the youngest of fifteen children.) I would just look at them in bewilderment. My father would say, when they left the house, "Girl, you didn't kill your mother. Your mother died of tuberculosis. You were just a beautiful little baby—and you looked just like your mother." Daddy wanted me to know he loved me and that I was not responsible for my mother's death. People would visit the house and talk about my mother. They'd say, "Oh, your mother was such a lady. She was such a saint!" So, I came to my own conclusions. Since Daddy thought I was so much like my mother, and people thought my mother was so wonderful, I put two and two together and decided—for myself—that maybe *I'm* wonderful, too! They say my mother would have given away her last cup of sugar, and so would I. I never knew her, but I always felt I was wonderful, just like her.

—PAULA WHARTON-LITT

A month after her death, I found the courage to sleep in Mama's bed. I wanted to feel her spirit, even prayed, insane woman that I had become, for an apparition or a voice . . . I felt nothing except pain.

—GLORIA WADE-GAYLES

From this valley they say you are going
we will miss your bright eyes and sweet smile,
for they say you are taking the sunshine
that has brightened our path for a while.

—FROM THE FUNERAL PROGRAM OF WILLIE MAE JEFFERSON,
1904–96, MOTHER OF TWELVE CHILDREN

I was finally crying over Mama. All of the talk about the holidays and parents had been the trigger. I remembered how just a year ago I'd wanted to be with her for the holidays but money and geography kept us apart. Now, I couldn't be with her because she was gone. The longing sense of loss finally became unbearable . . . Now that I had faced my grief and given into it, I felt like a burden had been lifted. I was finally ready to move on.

—JACKIE JOYNER-KERSEE

He is not hers, although she bore
For him a mother's pains;
He is not hers, although her blood
Is coursing through her veins!
He is not hers, for cruel hands
May rudely tear apart
The only wreath of household love
That binds her breaking heart.

—FRANCES WATKINS HARPER

The words flowed from my mouth, but I knew they were coming from someplace else. Someplace my mother had been the first to see in me. Someplace where she would live forever, strong and whole and beautiful again. That day, I sang as I've never sung before. This was a command performance . . . I was thirty-four years old, and for the first time I saw one of life's great truths with crystal clarity: A girl never really becomes a woman until she loses her mother.

—PATTI LABELLE, ON SINGING
AT HER MOTHER'S FUNERAL

Dear John:
Louisa fell asleep in my arms. I watch her face all through the moonshiny night. By dawn I was back in my den. And in two hours, I hear her say good-bye to neighbors and friends. The gate slammed, the stagecoach blew its horn, and my child was gone from sight.

—HARRIET TUBMAN, IN A LETTER TO HER BROTHER, JOHN

After distress, solace.

—SWAHILI PROVERB

Dear Mama, I am dying. I have all I want to eat, and I cannot eat it
. . . The doctor says I am homesick for you. I am six months with
child, and I have no strength for it and it is taking what little I have
for myself. I have made my bed, and now I must die in it. But I
cannot die without knowing you forgive me. Please come to me.

—FROM *THE WEDDING* BY DOROTHY WEST

My mother was forty-six when she died. The irony of it was that she was very athletic and in great shape. In fact, she'd just had a complete physical that June. On July 4, she went swimming with the family and mentioned casually that she felt like she had a cold coming on. She went back to the doctor, and this time they found a small spot on her lung. Still, the doctors were cautiously optimistic because they'd caught it early. In less than a week, though, further blood testing had revealed that the cancerous cells had been quicky carried to all parts of her body . . . So now you have this vibrant, beautiful woman—and you're being told she's going to be taken from you very quickly. And the doctors were right: Three months later, she was gone. On October 24, 1974, at 5:25 P.M., she passed away. My family and I were with her in the hospital when she took her last breath. Throughout her illness, we always kept a family vigil so that she was never alone. And even though she was in a coma, we talked to her; held her hand; told her funny stories. I was holding her hand when she took her last breath. It was a rainy, dreary day—the worst of the worst. But here is the light at the end of this rainbow: a miracle; a sign; or the everlasting presence of Mama. I visit her grave quite often. On one particularly gray, cold winter day, we went to put flowers on her grave. The skies were completely dark, even though it was the middle of the day. It was a cold, rainy, miserable day. But as we approached the cemetery, we noticed a gradual clearing of the clouds. As we entered the cemetery gates, the sunlight came through and lit the area where we were going, like a flashlight. We got out, laid the flowers, said a prayer, and got back in the car. Before we could get back out of the cemetery, the light was gone, the clouds reappeared, and the rain began again. If that's not everlasting love, then I don't know what is.

—RONNY B. LANCASTER

I was then put up to sale . . . The bidding commenced at a few pounds, and gradually rose to fifty-seven, when I was knocked down by the highest bidder; and the people who stood by said that I had fetched a great sum for so young a slave. I then saw my sisters led forth, and sold to different owners; so that we had not the sad satisfaction of being partners in bondage. When the sale was over, my mother hugged and kissed us, and mourned over us, begging of us to keep up a good heart, and do our duty to our new masters. It was a sad parting; one went one way, one another, and poor mammy went home with nothing.

—FROM "THE HISTORY OF MARY PRINCE," A SLAVE NARRATIVE

We aren't worried about dying one bit. We're hopeful that we'll get to Heaven. And won't it be the greatest pleasure to see Mama and Papa again? . . . Bessie told me recently, "Sadie, I think I'm going to die in my sleep. I think that sounds pretty good." And I said, "Good for *you*, maybe! But what about *me*!" I think that would be a mean thing for her to do to me. But you know, we aren't ready to give up yet, unless the Lord makes up His mind that it's finally time to call us. In the meantime, like all human beings, we want to keep on living. As Bessie says, "Heaven is my home but, honey, I ain't homesick!" When our time comes, we're going to be buried in the family plot in Raleigh. Bessie and I will be buried side by side—right next to Mama and Papa. We couldn't ask for anything more.

—SARAH DELANEY

When my mother passed, one of my dearest friends wrote me a letter which said, "When you lose your mother, there is nothing between you and eternity." And this is true. I've thought about it many times. There is an evolution of spiritual value that one gets once you get past the trauma of losing your mother. Does everybody find it? It largely depends on the mother-child relationship you had prior to losing this individual . . . You could either go on a guilt trip, or you could be rejuvenated and invigorated by recalling the many positive things that you did with this individual.

—NATALIA TANNER, M.D.

It stormed earlier tonight. Flashes of lightnin' lit up the attic room. I tried not to be scared. Lord, I miss Mama. When I was little and it would storm, me and Mama would hug up close and I wouldn't be scared.

The rain has finally stopped, but it is still hot, and muggy—cain't sleep. Besides, I woke up dreamin' bout Mama again . . . In my dream, I touched Mama's round, brown face. Like she used to do, she wet the tip of her apron and dabbed away the sweat over my upper lip and on my forehead. I saw myself readin' to her. She smiled and clapped her hands. I heard her soft voice praise me the way Mas' Henley do William when he gets li'l things right.

"I know so much more, Mama. Let me show you." . . . her face changed and her eyes held a warnin' I couldn't understand. "What's wrong, Mama?" She wanted to say somethin', but she was pulled away into the dark by some powerful big hand. "Mama, wait." She was gone, and I woke up to the cold, hurtin' truth. Mama is dead.

—PATRICIA MCKISSACK, *A PICTURE OF FREEDOM:*
THE DIARY OF CLOTEL, A SLAVE GIRL

At the hospital we almost ran to her room. She was lying on her back, breathing hard . . . she was staring at the ceiling but as soon as I came her eyes focused on me. I put my arms under her head and held her close to me. Her hand was shaking so hard the bed seemed to shudder.

"Mother, I'm here," I said to her. "We're here."

She was in her last transition of life and she was in a panic.

I watched her die. She died from the legs up. Suddenly her legs stopped shaking. They fell lifeless as the nurse lifted them. Then her hand lay still on the bed. I realized suddenly that I hadn't seen it still for over ten years. I continued to hold her hand. She continued to stare at me as she gasped for her last breath.

"Goodbye, Mother," Willemien said quietly.

It was the only sound in the room.

I stood quietly as I watched her leave me that day. It was the anniversary of my birth and now would be the anniversary of her death. But as I watched her die, I felt that the strength that left her body had entered mine. At that moment I received her final gift of inner empowerment. Her job of bringing love, peace and honor to the world now became mine.

—JOLIANA VAN OLPHEN-FEHR

My mother, Mattie Correll Cunningham, watches me. She died when I was not quite seven. I remember . . . my last sight of her alive: I was finishing breakfast and she was standing in the side doorway looking lovingly at me. She was dressed in her blue corduroy dressing gown. The day was cool and cloudy, and when I went outside I heard birds singing in the small oak tree outside our house. And then I remember the last time I saw her, in a coffin at home. She was wearing her best dress, made of pink satin. In her right hand was a single red rose. Roses were her favorite flower, and my daddy had planted them all around the house; big, deep-hued red roses. Ever since that day I have thought about her . . . Whenever I speak to young persons about the morality of the decisions they make in life, I usually tell them, "Don't do anything you couldn't tell your mother about."

—ARTHUR ASHE

I remember when my mother died, I went up to see her body, and I thought, who's that? For the first time I had some understanding of how extraordinary the concept of soul really is. Because that was not my mother. She wasn't moving, she wasn't talking, she wasn't doing anything, just gone. Where is that force? Does it evaporate? I don't think so. It continues. It just continues. She is with me right now, making sure I don't tell too many family secrets. It's nothing deep. She is just here with me.

—GEORGE C. WOLFE

My mother died October 3, 1993. We buried her on her birthday, October 5, 1993. She died very suddenly, and it was quite shocking. She lived with us in Chicago and, as far as I knew, had been in very good health. She had gone to visit relatives and check on a very sick aunt in Oklahoma when it happened.

I had talked to her the Friday before her death, and I remember I had taken the weekend off to go to our cabin in Michigan to write. We had a very long conversation—I remember every detail of the conversation and I cherish those details now—and the last thing she said to me before we hung up the phone was, "I love you." When she died the next day and I looked back on our last wonderful conversation, I realized that there wasn't really anything left unsaid between us. I couldn't have said goodbye any better than we did during our last conversation.

She didn't mention that she didn't feel well; in fact, she sounded like she was having a great time in Oklahoma, visiting with old school chums and relatives, as well as checking on her sick aunt. She was laughing and telling me about these long, wonderful visits she was having with all her old friends—some she hadn't seen since she was a little girl—and she was having a great time.

My mother had always said to me, when we'd just be talking casually, "Wherever I die, just bury me there. Don't carry my body across the country or take me all the way to Oklahoma to put me in the ground." She was always very practical and insisted that wherever she died, she just wanted to be buried there.

She was born in a tiny town called Goodnight, Oklahoma—and that's exactly where she died. She had traveled all over the world, had had a wonderfully productive, healthy life, then died in the place she was born. Her life had truly—literally—come full circle. We buried her there, of course.

It worked out as God would have wanted it—in an amazing way. When she died, I did not want to let her go. But I had no choice in the matter.

I remember thinking as soon as I got back to Chicago after the funeral, "Oh Lord, if I could just hold her hand *one more time*." It was just such a wish; such a strong wish . . . That night I went to sleep, and I dreamed that my mother and I were holding hands. The whole night, she was holding my hand. And when I awoke, I said to myself, "This is what I wished for—and what I asked for I received."

That experience was the beginning of my realization that my mother is still with me. She comes to me often, and she's with me all the time. I am no longer surprised or disoriented by these "mystical" events that let me know she's with me. It is what is real. It was what I know to be true—and I am completely comfortable with it.

Here's another way I know my mother walks with me still: The night she died I was in Michigan by myself—we have a little cottage there—and I had gone there to write. It's a very isolated setting, but I've always been comfortable there. For some reason, I just couldn't sleep that night. Finally, I dozed off, but it was a fitful sleep. In the middle of the night, I felt something next to my bed. I felt something touch me. I sat straight up in bed, terrorized, and then I sort of laughed at myself for being so jumpy and edgy that entire night . . .

A few minutes later, the phone rang and it was my husband telling me that they'd taken my mother to the hospital in Oklahoma. And now that I look back on it, I think that she had come to me—right then, at that moment of her death. At the moment she made her transition, she came to me. I felt like there was someone standing over me . . . It was a while before I realized that it was my mother who'd come to pay me a visit at the moment of her death. Maybe it was the breaking of a connection—but that isn't how it *felt*.

It felt as though there was someone there.

I shared these experiences with my husband and several close friends, and, although I know it sounds strange, they believe me.

Now let's progress to Christmas, and I'm in the kitchen cooking. Everyone has come from all over the country to be with me and support me during my first Christmas without my mother. I'm in the kitchen trying to put together the same kind of big meal that she and I used to make together. She made the best rolls, and I was always watching when she did it—but hers always tasted so much *better* that I never even tried to make the rolls myself. So here I am, trying to make my mother's rolls when I literally hear this voice—*her* voice—saying, "Renee, dump all of that out because you got your milk too hot and it burned the bottom and it killed off your yeast."

I told myself, "Okay, Renee. You are losing your mind. You're hearing voices, and that is the classic definition of schizophrenia.

You heard her voice speaking to you as clear as day. You're losing it, girl."

Immediately afterwards, I called a very close, elderly woman friend of mine named Mrs. Peterson. She listened very carefully and finally said, "Well, Renee . . . you need to understand that that *was* your mother and that she was in the kitchen with you. She will be there for you whenever you need her." And I said something like, "You mean I experienced a *memory* of the things she used to tell me about how to make rolls?" And she patiently said, "No, no . . . She was in the kitchen with you."

Mrs. Peterson was the one that pointed out to me that in many other cultures—especially the African culture—there are always salutes, ceremonies, and references to our ancestors, but they're not celebrating the *memory* of the deceased; they're celebrating the *presence* of our ancestors. Over time, I came to realize that Mrs. Peterson was exactly right: They are guardian angels or spirits—whatever you want to call them—and they are with us, present, all the time.

Death is a phenomenon of the body only. People who love you—especially your mother—never leave you. They stay around you forever.

So after I talked with Mrs. Peterson and tried to get myself together, I went back into the kitchen and tried to make the biscuits again. It was my mother that allowed me to go back in and finish cooking the meal and try not to cry too much into the food. After those and many other similar experiences—and after Mrs.

Peterson shared her age-old wisdom with me about death and dying—I must say that I was able, then, to forge a new relationship with my mother.

I am acutely aware of my mother's presence, and it gives me a tremendous sense of peace. I've evolved past that fresh, raw pain of grief and loss, and my mother and I have begun to forge a new relationship; a very warm, intense relationship. I know this all sounds rather strange, but I'm very sure of all of it. I'm sure some folks have probably said something like, "Oh, Renee is still just unwilling to 'let go' of her mother." But, in this case, they're *wrong*. In my mind, I don't see why you have to let go of the *spiritual* relationship anyway—why would you?

Believe me: There is something more than mere memory that exists after we lose a mother.

There definitely is between my mother and me; perhaps it is even deeper than when she walked this earth. After a while, this belief becomes intuitive—if you let it. You have to open yourself to it and let it *be*.

To African American women *and* men who have lost their mothers I can say this: After the grief has lifted a little, open your hearts and souls to the possibility that your mother's death does not mean complete loss. If you open yourselves to this idea, she will have even *more* power to influence your life, to heal you, and to calm you when you're troubled than she did when she walked on this earth.

I know my mother's body died. But her spirit did not. If you *want*

your mother in your life, she'll be there for you. You do not have to totally lose her, but you do have to be willing to forge a new and interesting kind of ongoing relationship with her. In order to do this, the first thing you have to believe is that your mother's spirit is still very much alive. You have to not only believe it, you have to *know* it.

The Western culture is so engrossed in the "if I can't see it and I can't touch it then it doesn't exist" attitude that we shut ourselves out of many life-altering and profound experiences. If you can let go of the feeling that all is lost, it will be revealed to you that all is *not* lost. So when miracles start to happen in your life, don't just chalk it up to coincidence; don't just say, "Ooooh, *that* was strange!" Understand that there is somebody intervening for you, and it is someone who loves you and is very close to you; and if you will open yourself up to them, you can have a real relationship with them.

No, it isn't the *same* earthly relationship, but it is a very powerful bond. That has now become my very vivid and clear understanding of the universe—and I am a very rational person. I mean, I'm an investigative reporter and have been for more than two decades. I deal every day with what *is*; with what we know we can document; with empirical evidence; with what really did happen. I spend my life and my career "cutting through the garbage" in an effort to get to truth, to get to fact. I don't pretend to know everything about the nature of the universe, but I do know that I have an amazingly wonderful relationship with my mother.

Kristin, there is no doubt in my mind that your mother is guiding you as you write this book, and that you were sent to me so that I could tell you this. Now I have told it to you.

And you must tell everybody.

—RENEE FERGUSON

We buried my mother in as much of a celebration of life as one can, because she was so full of life. After the grief, I struggled hard to find the positive in my mother's death, and I found it: First and foremost are the things I've retained; the spiritual connection. Yes, I lost the physical connection, but I found something else. I know now that the spiritual connection between a mother and child is very special. For me, that remains in place. Second, I have the memories. In our daily lives, my sisters and I make reference to her all the time—"you know Ma would have said to wash your mouth out with soap for saying that." I talk to her myself when I'm facing a difficult time; I say, "Mama, give me strength." I remember her in prayer. These are ways of keeping her alive with me. It is a manifestation to me that our bond is still in place. The memories serve as wonderful reminders of the richness of the times we had together, but they also serve as guideposts for how to live your life, and how parents should teach their children how to live their lives: living a life of integrity, caring for your family, helping others, doing the right thing. These are many of the lessons that I am now trying to pass on to my own daughter.

—RONNY B. LANCASTER

Blessed are those who mourn,
for they will be comforted.

—MATTHEW 5:4

I lay down in my grave
and watch my children
grow proud blooms
above the weeds of death.

—MAYA ANGELOU

This photo is symbolic to me because it was so typical of how my mother treated me as an equal, as a friend; always looking at me at eye level, even if she had to lift me up and place me on the banister so that we could look each other eye to eye, face to face.

—RENEE FERGUSON

You have turned my mourning into dancing.

—PSALMS 30:11

Travel through the grief—slowly if you have to—then gradually arrive on the other side where the sun is bright and our spiritual mothers stand, replete with their everlasting love, welcoming us with open arms.

$\mathscr{P}$HOTO $\mathscr{C}$REDITS

Page iv. Mother teaching her child to read. © Jason Miccolo Johnson.

Page vii. Lonnie Paul, Lonnie Paul II, and Mary Elizabeth Taylor. Courtesy of Kristin Clark Taylor.

Page 7. Woman with infant. Reproduced from the Collections of the Library of Congress. LC US262 122998.

Page 11. Pregnant woman. © Jason Miccolo Johnson.

Page 13. Woman in white dress with infant. Reproduced from the Collections of the Library of Congress LC USF34 54159E.

Page 15. Kristin Clark Taylor with son Lonnie Paul and newborn Mary Elizabeth. Courtesy of Kristin Clark Taylor.

Page 16. Left to right: Ruth Smith Vincent, Marilyn Sanders Thomas, Martha Horner Roberts, Heather Vincent Holley (baby), Martha Sanders Vincent, and Martha Roberts Sanders. Courtesy of Heather Vincent Holley.

Page 17. Martha Horner Roberts with her children, Elizabeth Roberts Pruitt and Martha Roberts Sanders. Courtesy of Heather Vincent Holley.

Page 20. Couple with their newborn on front porch. Reproduced from the Collections of the Library of Congress LC US262 122973.

Page 27. Mother holding her baby in her Sunday best, with second child standing. © Jason Miccolo Johnson.

Page 30. Black family in church. Reproduced from the Collections of the Library of Congress LC USF34 46349D.

Page 33. Son sleeping on mother's lap in church. © Jason Miccolo Johnson.

Page 34. Mary Elizabeth Clark. Courtesy of Kristin Clark Taylor.

Page 39. Women in church with arms stretched high. Reproduced from the Collections of the Library of Congress LC USF34 887642.

Page 44. Kristin Clark Taylor with mother, Mary Elizabeth Clark, and newborn Lonnie Paul at his christening. Courtesy of Kristin Clark Taylor.

Pages 45 and 49. Mother holding infant with young daughter standing by. Reproduced from the Collections of the Library of Congress LC USF33 21391M3.

Pages 52 and 60. Mother on front porch surrounded by her five children. Reproduced from the Collections of the Library of Congress LC USW3 1904C.

Page 57. Lola Keyes with her mother, Anna Bryant, her daughter, Lola Elizabeth, and her son, William A. (B. J.) Keyes. Courtesy of Lola Keyes.

Page 59. Yvette Richardson with her children, Lynn and James. Courtesy of Lynn Richardson.

Page 65. Mother at front door holding her baby, smaller child standing at her side. Reproduced from the Collections of the Library of Congress LC US262 11291M.

Page 67. Stone bridge. Reproduced from the Collections of the Library of Congress LC US262 122974.

Page 68. Daughter resting on her mother's shoulder in church. © Jason Miccolo Johnson.

Page 73. Woman baking biscuits. © Jason Miccolo Johnson.

Page 75. Kristin Clark Taylor with son Lonnie Paul. Courtesy of Kristin Clark Taylor.

Page 79. Mother with six children peering out window. Reproduced from the Collections of the Library of Congress LC US262 122999.

Page 82. Anna W. Randolph. Courtesy of Laura Randolph.

Page 85. Lonnie Taylor with his mother, Magdalene Sturges Taylor. Courtesy of Kristin Clark Taylor.

Page 87. Elizabeth Hunter and her daughter, Charlotte. Courtesy of Charlotte Hunter.

Page 89. Mother teaching her children at home. Reproduced from the Collections of the Library of Congress LC USF34 TO1 31938.

Page 90. Mary Elizabeth Clark surrounded by her children on her graduation day. Courtesy of Kristin Clark Taylor.

Page 92. Elderly woman. © Jason Miccolo Johnson.

Page 98. One-hundred-year-old woman teaching herself how to write. Reproduced from the Collections of the Library of Congress LC US262 46748.

Page 100. Magdalene Sturges graduating from high school at the age of fifteen. Courtesy of Magdalene S. Taylor.

Page 102. Mother reading to her children. Reproduced from the Collections of the Library of Congress LC USW3 390C.

Page 112. The Bing sisters. Courtesy of Magdalene Sturges Taylor.

Page 115. Lonnie Paul Taylor II. Courtesy of Kristin Clark Taylor.

Page 117. Several generations standing outside. Courtesy of Kristin Clark Taylor.

Page 122. Magdalene Sturges Taylor, mother of fourteen children (eleven biological and three adoptive). Courtesy of Magdalene Sturges Taylor.

Page 125. Magdalene Sturges Taylor and her children. Courtesy of Magdalene Sturges Taylor.

Page 126. Magdalene Sturges Taylor with Talonda, Talaya, and Lotoria, her adoptive daughters, and her granddaughter, Mary Elizabeth, in Snow White costume. Courtesy of Kristin Clark Taylor.

Page 129. Mary Wright. Courtesy of Phyllis Armstrong.

Page 136. Kristin Clark with older sister, Noelle Clark. Courtesy of Kristin Clark Taylor.

Page 137. Joetta Elizabeth Tobin. Courtesy of Ronny B. Lancaster.

Page 138. Mary Elizabeth Clark featured on front page of *Pittsburgh Courier*. Courtesy of Kristin Clark Taylor.

Page 141. Myra Lou Kent. Courtesy of Phyllis Armstrong.

Page 143. Zeolar Powell. Courtesy of Phyllis Armstrong .

Page 144. Mary Elizabeth Clark. Courtesy of Kristin Clark Taylor.

Page 147. Photography by Cecil O'Neil Walters.

Page 151. Corine Sturges. Courtesy of Magdalene Sturges Taylor.

Page 153. Ena Parker with her children, Allen Lyfrock, Salome Lyfrock, Esther Parker, and Alice Ramessar. Courtesy of Patricia Blythe.

Page 157. Hettie Walker. Courtesy of Richard Cheppy.

Page 163. Woman surrounded by photos. © Jason Miccolo Johnson.

Page 165. Digital image. Copyright. © 1999 by PhotoDisc, Inc.

Page 169. Portrait of five generations of mothers. Reproduced from the Collections of the Library of Congress LC US262 161928.

Page 170. Natalia Tanner Cain, M.D., and her grandson, Tanner Oliver Long. Courtesy of Dr. Natalia Tanner.

Page 173. Mary Prater, former slave, at one hundred years old. Reproduced from the Collections of the Library of Congress LC US262 11077.

Page 179. Kristin Clark Taylor with her mother, Mary Elizabeth Clark, her mother-in-law, Magdalene S. Taylor, and her infant son, Lonnie Paul Taylor II.

Page 185. Mary Elizabeth Sorsby with her grandson, Lonnie Paul Taylor II. Courtesy of Kristin Clark Taylor II.

Page 187. Women at graveside. Reproduced from the Collections of the Library of Congress LC USF33 11875.

Page 205. Digital image. Copyright © 1999 by PhotoDisc, Inc.

Page 212. Woman and daughter lay wreath at graveside. © Jason Miccolo Johnson.

Page 216. Renee Ferguson and her mother, Mary. Courtesy of Renee Ferguson.

About the Author

Kristin Clark Taylor is the author of *Black Fathers: A Call for Healing* and *The First to Speak: A Woman of Color Inside the White House*, a memoir of her experiences as the first African American woman in history to have held the senior post of White House Director of Media Relations. A former journalist, she was a member of *USA Today*'s creation and launch team and worked as an editorial board member, columnist, and writer. A former corporate public relations executive for two Fortune 500 companies, she is now an author, lecturer, and communications consultant. She lives in Washington, D.C., and is currently completing her fourth book.